The Hows and Whys of Fluency Instruction

Melanie R. Kuhn
Boston University

Boston   New York   San Francisco
Mexico City   Montreal   Toronto   London   Madrid   Munich   Paris
Hong Kong   Singapore   Tokyo   Cape Town   Sydney

Executive Editor: Aurora Martínez Ramos
Series Editorial Assistant: Kara Kikel
Marketing Manager: Krista Clark
Production Editor: Gregory Erb
Editorial Production Service: DB Production Services, Inc.
Composition Buyer: Linda Cox
Manufacturing Buyer: Megan Cochran
Electronic Composition: Schneck-DePippo Graphics
Cover Designer: Linda Knowles

For Professional Development resources visit www.allynbaconmerrill.com

Between the time website information is gathered and then published, it is not unusual for some sites to have closed. Also, the transcription of URLs can result in typographical errors. The publisher would appreciate notification where these errors occur so that they may be corrected in subsequent editions.

Library of Congress Cataloging-in-Publication Data
Kuhn, Melanie R.
  The hows and whys of fluency instruction / Melanie R. Kuhn.
    p. cm.
  Includes bibliographical references and index.
  ISBN-13: 978-0-205-54216-1 (alk. paper)
  ISBN-10: 0-205-54216-6 (alk. paper)
  1. Oral reading. 2. Fluency (Language learning) 3. Reading (Primary) I. Title.

LB1573.5.K86 2008
372.45′2—dc22   2008026240

Printed in the United States of America

10 9 8 7 6 5 4 3 2 1   RRD-VA 12 11 10 09 08

**Allyn & Bacon
is an imprint of**

www.pearsonhighered.com   ISBN-10: 0-205-54216-6
                            ISBN-13: 978-0-205-54216-1

*To the teachers who are committed to
creating a better world through education and
the students who will make that world possible*

*And to the memory of my father, Raymond Kuhn,
and my mentor and friend, Steven Stahl*

Contents

Preface

When I began my work on fluency in the late '90s, it was definitely not a "hot topic" (Cassidy & Cassidy, 2007, p. 1); since then, things have changed quite dramatically—and for good reason. Fluency is a critical component of the reading process, allowing your students to make the transition between monotonous, purposeful decoding and automatic, expressive reading (National Reading Panel, 2000). Because of this, it is important that you include instruction designed to assist learners in making this transition within your literacy curriculum. While a number of highly effective strategies for developing fluent reading exist, it is necessary to consider how well each fits into your particular classroom setting. Are you working with an entire class of second or third graders who are making the transition to fluent reading? Or do you have a small number of older students, say fourth grade and above, who are experiencing difficulty becoming fluent? I have designed this book to provide you with approaches to fluency instruction that are appropriate for each of these situations. Further, the methods that I present are grounded in research *and* have been shown to be effective in practice. They include instructional strategies for individual readers, pairs of learners, and flexible groups as well as whole classes of students. They help you to employ oral reading effectively, often using texts that are more complex than those your students can read independently, without reverting to round-robin reading (or its more recent iterations of popcorn, combat, or popsicle reading).

In order to help determine which of your students will benefit from fluency instruction, I present a chapter on assessment strategies early in the book. These assessments are relatively easy to apply and serve two purposes. First, they allow you to determine whether you need to focus on fluency as part of your literacy curriculum—and with which students. Second, they are an authentic means of monitoring your students' fluency development. By periodically looking at the oral reading of your learners, you can decide whether their fluency is developing at a reasonable rate or whether you need to integrate specific fluency-oriented strategies into your reading instruction or as part of their independent practice (for example, incorporating a reading-while-listening approach [Chomsky, 1976] during their independent reading time).

It is also important to discuss why a focus on fluency is deserving of your valuable class time. If fluency instruction's only purpose were to create faster, more expressive readers, it might be worth a bit of your class time but it would not be the most efficient expenditure of your instructional efforts. However, fluency plays a vital role in your students' ability to construct meaning from text and as such is an essential component of your learners' literacy development (Kuhn & Stahl, 2003). Fluency affects your students' ability to understand what they are reading in two ways. First, fluent readers can recognize words both accurately and automatically. By developing automatic word recognition, your students are able to focus on the meaning of the text rather than on the identification of the words themselves. Second, by using appropriate expression, your students are demonstrating their capacity to determine shades of meaning as they read, an ability that gains importance as their reading material becomes increasingly complex. Given this, ensuring that your students are able to make the transition to fluent reading is well worth your while.

While a basic understanding of "how words work" is a prerequisite to fluent reading, it is important to mention that this book does not focus on word recognition instruction per se. Similarly, while comprehension is a central outcome of fluent reading, this book does not focus on comprehension instruction, either. Rather, its emphasis is on strategies that can help students make the transition to fluent reading, a process that allows their word recognition to become automatic, their reading to become expressive, and, ultimately, their focus to be on the construction of meaning from text.

In order to present this information in a coherent way, I have laid out the book in the following way:

Chapter 1 discusses the components of fluent reading, its role in the reading process, and principles for effective oral reading instruction.

Chapter 2 provides ways of assessing your learners' fluency development.

Chapter 3 presents fluency approaches that can be used as the basis of your whole-class (shared) reading instruction.

Chapter 4 talks about methods of fluency instruction designed for flexible grouping.

Chapter 5 focuses on fluency instruction for pairs and individual learners.

Chapter 6 looks at strategies that can serve as supplemental instruction for your overall literacy curriculum.

An addendum lists award-winning challenging texts.

Given the importance of challenging texts in the fluency development of all learners, I felt it was critical to provide a resource for newer teachers who are attempting to build classroom libraries for their budding fluent readers. The research and reasoning behind each instructional approach is also presented in the chapters, along with a "Lesson Snapshot" that provides guidelines for implementing these methods in your classroom.

While the activities presented in each chapter are designed for particular types of instructional groups, most can be adapted for use with alternative grouping formats with minimal effort on your part. As such, you can use these strategies with learners across grade levels, from developing readers in second and third grade to struggling readers in high school. I hope you will find this format useful and my suggestions both practical and easy to implement. By using effective instructional tools such as those presented in this book, it is possible to help students become fluent and engaged readers, thereby laying the groundwork for a lifetime of independent reading.

Acknowledgments

I would like to thank: my husband, Jason Chambers; my mother, Emma Kuhn; my friend James Costa; my mentors Paula Schwanenflugel and Lesley Morrow; and Aurora Martínez and Kara Kikel at Allyn & Bacon. Without their love, support, and assistance, this book would not be possible.

This book was supported in part by the Interagency Education Research Initiative, a program of research jointly managed by the National Science Foundation (Grant No. 0089258), the Institute of Education Sciences in the U.S. Department of Education, and the National Institute of Child Health and Human Development in the National Institutes of Health (National Institutes of Health Grant No. 7 R01 HD040746-06).

I would also like to thank the following reviewers for their comments and suggestions: Deborah Adbo, Palm Beach Atlantic University; Mary Cockerille, Walker Upper Elementary School; Rose Marie Codling, University of Maryland; Amy Ely, Brush Schools; Sallie Averitt Miller, Columbus State University; and Pamela Tow, Franklin-Edison School.

Chapter 1

What Is Fluent Reading and Why Is It Important?

Instructional Approach	Grade Levels	Grouping	Type of Text
Echo Reading	Any grade level	Any teacher-directed grouping format (e.g., can be integrated into whole-class, small-group, or tutoring formats)	• Challenging texts
Choral Reading	Any grade level	Any teacher-directed grouping format (e.g., can be integrated into whole-class, small-group, or tutoring formats)	• Repeated reading of a longer, challenging text • Shorter instructional level texts (e.g., poems, speeches, passages from longer texts)
Partner Reading	Any grade level	Any grouping format (can be used as part of whole-class, small-group, or tutoring formats; could also be used in centers)	• Challenging texts if previously read • Instructional level or independent level texts if previously unread

■ What is fluency's role in the reading process?

■ How has oral reading's role in the literacy curriculum changed?

■ Are there general principles of effective fluency instruction?

Where Does Fluency Fit in a Child's Reading Development?

A friend of mine recently mentioned that she was curious about the path her child's reading development had followed. When her daughter, Rebecca,[1] was in kindergarten, she loved being read to and would listen to certain stories over and over. Eventually, Rebecca memorized her favorites, "reading" them to anyone who was willing to listen. What perplexed my friend was that her daughter sounded quite fluent when she shared these stories in kindergarten, but when she entered first grade her reading suddenly became less fluent. Instead of reading smoothly, Rebecca grappled with words she didn't recognize in texts that were less predictable or familiar than her "old" favorites had been. It was only over the course of second and, now, third grade that Rebecca's reading began to sound fluent again. Rebecca is quite a good student; however, my friend was wondering if her daughter's experience was an unusual one. I assured her that it is quite common for learners to make such transitions and that students' reading development makes several qualitative shifts over the course of their schooling.

Unlike my friend, as an educator, you expect students' reading to move through different phases throughout their school years (Chall, 1996). Although the understanding and enjoyment of texts should always be the ultimate goal of reading instruction, students' comfort with written material varies widely depending on their development level. In general, **emergent readers** are developing **concepts of print**, familiarity with text (e.g., **book-handling knowledge**), and **phonemic awareness** (Teale & Sulzby, 1986; Yopp & Yopp, 2000). Having established this, the emphasis in first grade shifts to **word recognition** (Adams, 1990). As students develop familiarity with **letter-sound correspondence** and begin to build their **sight word** vocabulary, the focus in second and third grade shifts again to fluent reading. At this point, in addition to accuracy, readers should begin to develop automaticity and prosody, or the use of appropriate phrasing and expression (Kuhn & Stahl, 2003). By integrating fluency instruction into your literacy curriculum during these grades, you can help your learners make the transition from hesitant, word-by-word reading to reading that is smooth and expressive.

Beyond the primary grades, it is assumed that most readers have established a certain level of **fluency**, at least when it comes to reading grade-level material. Ideally, by the time students reach the fourth grade, they are making the transition from learning to read to reading to learn (Chall, 1996); their texts become increasingly complex, and there is a significant shift toward content-area literacy. Unfortunately, some learners never quite establish the transition to fluent reading; instead, their reading remains slow, choppy, and expressionless far past the third grade. This lack of fluency interferes with both the pleasure students derive from their reading and their ability to learn from text. If this is the case for some of your students, targeted fluency instruction is likely to help them become skilled readers. The chapters in this book address students at both ends of the spectrum; that is, students who are making the transition to fluency at what we consider to be a developmentally appropriate point (i.e., second and third grade) and students who have experienced difficulty with this transition (i.e., students in fourth grade and beyond). There will also be tables indicating the range of grade levels, grouping formats, and types of text that are appropriate for each strategy.

What Is Fluency and Why Is It Important?

Fluent readers share a range of characteristics; their **fluent reading** is smooth, effortless, and expressive (Kuhn & Stahl, 2003). In other words, fluent readers have developed the ability to recognize words automatically as well as accurately, and they can incorporate the use of appropriate phrasing and expression into their reading. All these elements indicate that the person reading is comfortable with the text at hand. As stated earlier, however, if fluency were simply a surface-level issue, one that ensured automatic and expressive oral reading on the part of your students, it would be worth expending some class time on, but probably would not be worthy of your extensive instructional efforts. But fluency is actually considered by many to be a bridge between decoding and comprehension (Pikulski & Chard, 2005); its instruction deserves a significant role in the literacy curriculum (National Reading Panel, 2000).

So how, exactly, does fluency contribute to a reader's ability to comprehend text? I would argue that it does so in two ways, both of which build on its defining components: accurate, automatic word recognition and the appropriate use of prosodic, or expressive, features such as stress, pitch, or suitable phrasing.

The Role of Accuracy

Accuracy is key to fluency. If students are to make sense of what they read, it is necessary that they accurately identify the vast majority of words they encounter in text (e.g., Chall, 1996; National Reading Panel, 2000). In order to do so, students must determine the relationship that exists between letters (or groups of letters, such as *sh*) and the sounds that those letters make. Similarly, they need to be able to identify **high-frequency words** without having to decode them (words that occur frequently in texts, such as *this*, *of*, and *when*). When students begin to read, they often appear to be overly focused on identifying every word they encounter, a process that makes their reading sound stilted and uneven. It is the role of decoding instruction[2], and of instruction in word recognition more broadly, to assist students in generalizing their understandings about letters, words, and word families, thereby allowing them to more easily recognize the words they encounter in print.[3] But, while such accuracy is critical to comprehension, it is not enough. In fact, students who are accurate but deliberate in their word recognition not only sound disfluent, they are unlikely to be able to construct meaning from text. In order to do so, it is critical that students develop their **automaticity** as well.

The Role of Automaticity

The significance of automatic word recognition in the reading process becomes clear when you visualize children's early attempts at reading. As mentioned earlier, first graders frequently expend significant amounts of effort trying to figure out the words that compose a given sentence, leaving them with little or no attention remaining to determine its meaning. As a result, by the time they have reached the end of a sentence, they have no idea what it was about—even though they would have easily understood it had someone read it to them. Unfortunately, older struggling readers who have yet to make the transition to automatic word recognition often experience the same difficulties.

The problems readers encounter as the result of slow word recognition can best be explained through *automaticity theory* (e.g., LaBerge & Samuels, 1974; Logan, 1997), which states that individuals have a limited amount of attention available for any complex task. When we encounter activities that are comprised of multiple components, it is difficult for us to focus fully on each aspect of these activities simultaneously. In order to deal effectively with such complex activities, it is necessary for certain aspects of those tasks to become effortless or automatic. In the case of reading, higher-order processes such as comprehension are underpinned by the need to correctly decode what is written.[4] So if we are to be able to focus on meaning, we need to make our decoding automatic.

The question becomes: How do learners go about developing such automatic decoding? The answer lies in practice. As with any new skill, from learning to play basketball to learning to play an instrument, the only way to progress from novice to expert is through practice. In terms of reading, this means ensuring that learners have extensive exposure to print in order to develop their comfort with the spelling patterns, or orthography, that comprise written English. In other words, in order to develop automatic word recognition, learners need to spend significant amounts of time reading. And, while word recognition instruction is an essential component of such practice, if students are to become fluent readers, it is critical that they also have the opportunity to apply their developing knowledge to the reading of **connected text** such as books, poems, or newspapers. Without such practice, there is no guarantee that what they have learned about how words work in isolation will transfer to their reading; on the other hand, when given plentiful opportunities to read—with appropriate support where necessary—the likelihood that learners will develop automaticity increases significantly.

The Role of Prosody

The final component of fluent reading has a more complex relationship to comprehension. **Prosody** incorporates those aspects of oral reading that allow it to sound expressive, including pitch or intonation, stress or emphasis, tempo or rate, and the rhythmic patterns of language (e.g., Erekson, 2003; Kuhn & Stahl, 2003). According to Lynn Truss (2004), prosodic elements in written text are regularly represented by punctuation. She argues that "punctuation directs you how to read, in the way musical notation directs a musician how to play" (p. 20). The importance of appropriate punctuation in the meaning of a sentence can be demonstrated by the joke that appears on the back cover of her book:

A panda walks into a café. He orders a sandwich, eats it, then draws a gun and fires two shots in the air.

"Why?" asks the confused waiter, as the panda makes towards the exit. The panda produces a badly punctuated wild-life manual and tosses it over his shoulder.

"I'm a panda," he says, at the door. "Look it up."

The waiter turns to the relevant entry and, sure enough, finds an explanation.

"*Panda.* Large black-and-white bear-like mammal, native to China. Eats, shoots and leaves."

The degree to which this definition becomes muddled simply as the result of one incorrect comma is remarkable.

Unfortunately, many attributes that represent prosody in conversation, such as the fluctuation of a speaker's voice or the correct phrasing, don't directly translate to print. For example, while phrase units can sometimes be identified through the use of commas, this is not always the case (e.g., Miller & Schwanenflugel, 2006), and inappropriate breaks in a sentence can often interfere with a learner's understanding of the text. For example, if you were to read a sentence in two-word groupings, you would likely have to work harder to determine the meaning. Take a look at the following excerpt, taken from *Alice in Wonderland* (Carroll, 2006):

> Alice was   beginning to   get very   tired of   sitting by
> her sister   on the   bank and   of having   nothing to
> do: once   or twice she had   peeped into   the book   her sister
> was reading   but it   had no   pictures or   conversations in
> it, and   "what is   the use   of a   book," thought
> Alice, "without   pictures or   conversations?" (p. 1)

It is likely to be a bit difficult for you as a fluent reader not to jump over these breaks in order to make sense of the passage. However, such inappropriate phrasing often occurs in disfluent reading, and the lack of correctly phrased units, or **parsing**, can negatively impact comprehension. The good news is that many studies (e.g., Cromer,

1970; Casteel, 1988; Weiss, 1983) show that poor readers at all age levels demonstrate improved comprehension when text is presented in a manner that replicates speech; that is, when it has been organized into appropriate phrase units for them.

In order to tie these findings to fluent reading, I would argue that if fluent readers read aloud not only at a reasonable pace and with relatively few miscues but also with expression or in a manner that replicates oral language, they are also prosodic readers. And if, as the previous discussion indicates, prosodic readers are better able to comprehend text than their nonprosodic peers, then it seems reasonable to assert that fluent readers are better able to construct meaning from text than are disfluent readers. As such, by helping learners become fluent readers, we are aiding not only their ability to automatically decode and read with expression but also their ability to construct meaning from text.

Before leaving the issue of prosody, it is important to mention one caveat. While most researchers would agree that automaticity plays a role in a reader's comprehension, the exact relationship between prosody and comprehension is less clear (e.g., Kuhn et al., 2006). There are three possible explanations for this relationship: One is that readers need to have an understanding of what is being read before they can read it prosodically. The second is that readers must determine the prosodic elements of what is being read before they are able to understand it. And the third, which represents my position, is that prosody both reflects and contributes to readers' understanding of text. Ideally, as we learn more about fluency, we will better clarify this issue. In the meantime, whatever relationship exists between these two components of skilled reading, it is important to emphasize appropriate expression in the reading curriculum, both because a relationship between prosody and comprehension does exist and because the use of appropriate phrasing and expression are critical to a reader's enjoyment of a given text.

Oral Reading Then and Now

One issue that usually arises when discussing fluency has to do with the value of oral reading in the literacy curriculum. The value of this practice hinges, to a large extent, on what is meant by the term. If, by oral reading, you mean instruction that is comprised primarily or exclusively of round-robin reading or its virtual equivalents, popcorn, popsicle, or combat reading, then it is unlikely you will be able to further the reading development of your learners. If, on the other hand, you envision oral reading practice as involving a range of effective reading strategies—from repeated reading to Wide Reading Instruction—you will likely be successful at assisting your learners in becoming fluent readers. In the latter case, oral reading clearly deserves a place in your curriculum.

Round-Robin Reading—
An All-Too-Common Experience

Given that round-robin reading and its equivalents are nearly omnipresent in our schools, it is necessary to discuss what constitutes these procedures, along with how and why they came to be the dominant forms of oral reading instruction. **Round-robin reading** requires that every student in a group or a classroom read a small portion of the material currently being covered, usually a few sentences or a paragraph. It is often used as part of the literacy curriculum, but is equally popular in the content-area classroom. There are a number of reasons touted for using this approach (Ash & Kuhn, 2006), including to make difficult material accessible, to ensure that each student reads at least a portion of the text, to assess students' oral reading development, to help with classroom management, and to develop students' fluency.

Despite the range of potential attributes that make round-robin reading look effective on the surface, the procedure fails on all counts. To begin with, while having each student read a section of the text in order to cover difficult material seems to make sense, it does little toward creating a unified rendering of a selection. Instead, it takes a single text and creates a number of dissonant parts. Further, since each reader is concentrating on part of a text rather than the text as a whole, such reading is likely to focus students away from the meaning of the passage and toward word identification instead.

While requiring each student to read a section of text ensures that everyone has covered at least a small portion of the material, this is unlikely to increase learners' reading ability—for two reasons: First, in terms of time expended, this format allows learners to read only between one and three minutes per day (Gambrell, 1984), not nearly enough time for students to become skilled readers (e.g., Allington, 1977; Shanahan, 2007). Second, if students are to read in front of their peers, it is important that they have the opportunity to practice the material beforehand so they can present themselves in the best possible light.

When students are forced to read an unpracticed text aloud, you will find that while some may perform well, many others will sound like disfluent or disengaged readers. And though this variation in reading ability seems to give you insight into your students' reading development, several factors may skew an accurate evaluation. For example, if students are nervous reading in front of their peers, their rendering may appear less skilled. Similarly, students may disengage with the text since they are only responsible for a small section of the material and, as a result, may not read as well. It is also possible that the material used for whole-class instruction is either too easy or too difficult for some of your readers, which may affect how fluent your students sound.

As for classroom management, it may seem that by asking each of your students to read a portion of the text you are helping them engage with the material, thereby increasing their time on task. In reality, it is more likely that this procedure actually decreases the amount of attention they pay to their reading. Some students will try to determine which passage they will be reading aloud and then practice that section to themselves in an attempt to sound competent in front of their peers. Once they have had their turn, they breathe a sigh of relief and proceed to tune out until they think their next turn is approaching. Other readers, who most need to practice identifying unfamiliar words, rarely get the opportunity to do so because their more skilled peers regularly "jump in" with the correct word—either in an attempt to be helpful or simply because they become impatient waiting. On the other hand, some students become so engaged with the text that they begin to read at their own pace rather than following along with the class, "losing their place" in the process. When their teacher discovers that they are not following along with the class, they are often reprimanded and asked to slow down in order to keep pace with their peers. Since it is extremely difficult for many readers to slow down their reading speed, these learners become bored with the entire process and disengage from the text.

Finally, there is the notion that round-robin reading helps learners develop fluency. But, since students are only responsible for reading small portions of connected text as part of this procedure, they do not have sufficient opportunities to develop into skilled readers.

Because of these negatives, round-robin reading has metamorphosed into three supposedly alternative approaches—popcorn, popsicle, and combat reading—that are designed to correct at least one of its failings: the lack of attention students pay to the text when it is not their turn to read. Students who participate in round-robin reading usually read in a predetermined order; as a result, they often spend time determining which passage they will be reading, practicing that passage, then tuning out once they have completed their turn. The three alternatives differ from the original in one notable way, their approach to student selection. In **popcorn reading**, students are randomly selected and, as with kernels popping in a popper, it is uncertain who will be chosen next. In **popsicle reading**, students' names are written on popsicle sticks, which are then placed in a bag and selected at random by the teacher. In **combat reading**, students are assigned the task of selecting the next reader, with classmates who are not paying attention being the preferred target. However, despite the possibility that students may be somewhat more focused on the text as the result of these changes, the approaches do nothing to address the remaining issues and, overall, have similar results to round-robin reading.

The Changing Role of Oral Reading

Now you may wonder, why, given all these negatives, is round-robin reading so commonly used? To understand that, it is necessary to look at the history of reading instruction in the United States. According to Jim Hoffman (1987) and Tim Rasinski (2006), one of the primary purposes of reading instruction prior to the 1900s was to emphasize students' ability to recite a text expressively, either to share information or as a form of entertainment. The reason behind this was twofold. First, since many, if not most, jobs at this time required little reading or writing, education in America was not universal, and, where offered, was unlikely to be as comprehensive as it is today. As a result, far fewer individuals were literate. Second, written materials were not as plentiful as they are now, and those that did exist, especially books, were relatively expensive. In fact, the only book in many homes was the Bible, and many families could not even afford that. As a result, a limited number of individuals in any community, usually members of government, religious leaders, and professionals, were responsible for relaying text-based information to their less literate peers, often by reading a text aloud. Given the importance of conveying information to others in this manner, it was critical that literacy instruction stressed the oral interpretation of texts.

As universal education took hold and materials became increasingly available, reading for private purposes came to be regarded as the norm. Rather than reading aloud to family members in the parlor or to fellow citizens in the public square, individuals were likely to pick up a penny novel, comic book, or newspaper and read to themselves. This shift in reading led to a parallel shift in literacy instruction away from reading for oral performance and toward reading silently to meet individual needs and created a dilemma: when students are reading silently, it is difficult to determine whether they are learning what is being taught—or even if they are reading at all.

In order to find out exactly what students were doing as they read a particular text, teachers began a process of randomly checking on students as they were reading silently to see whether they were developing word recognition, making progress in the text, and completing their assignment. Eventually, this random checking evolved into the procedure known as round-robin reading, and it became the norm. While originating from a set of valid concerns, this approach simply is not an effective way to help develop skilled readers. The question then becomes, What can you replace it with? While the rest of the book presents a range of instructional approaches that have been shown to be effective alternatives to round-robin reading, both in research and in practice (e.g., Kuhn & Stahl, 2003; National Reading Panel, 2000), I want to end this chapter by presenting four general principles (Rasinski, 2003) and three instructional approaches designed to support your students' fluency development and easily integrated into your day-to-day oral reading instruction.

What Makes for Effective Fluency Instruction?

As a teacher, you can easily incorporate four principles designed to promote fluent reading into your literacy instruction (Rasinski, 2003). The first is modeling expressive reading. This is perhaps one of the best ways to instill a love of reading in your students while providing them with a sense of what good reading should sound like. While this practice is quite common in the early primary grades, it becomes increasingly rare as students get older. Nevertheless, a substantial body of literature is best presented as spoken word, from poems and plays to highly descriptive narratives and gripping pieces of nonfiction. By taking five minutes or so each day to read a text, you are creating a shared experience for the class. You are also offering your students the chance to hear what fluent reading sounds like. And by making the effort to present a range of genres during this period, you are increasing the likelihood your students will recognize that reading provides something of interest for virtually everyone.

As positive an activity as this can be, it is important to stress that it should be only a small portion of your class's day. If too much of your class time is spent reading aloud to your students, they will not have the opportunities necessary to develop their own reading skills. And while it may seem as though this is an effective way of dealing with difficult material, it is important that your learners have the opportunity to read some challenging texts—especially those in the content areas—themselves, provided they are given sufficient scaffolding. Otherwise, they are unlikely to develop the ability to read this type of material—exactly the opposite of what you would want for them.

The second and third principles—offering learners extensive opportunities to practice reading connected text and providing sufficient support and assistance—help students make the transition to fluent reading by giving them a great deal of practice consolidating what they know about word recognition. Similarly, when learners are faced with challenging material containing a high percentage of unknown words or new vocabulary or concepts, it is essential that support is available to aid them with their reading. This support can be as simple as integrating echo or choral reading into your literacy lessons, or it can entail a reworking of the shared reading component of your curriculum using an approach such as Fluency Oral Reading Instruction or the Wide Fluency Oral Reading Instruction (see Chapter 3 for a description).

The fourth principle is emphasizing appropriate phrasing as part of your oral reading lessons. This principle builds on the notions of modeling and support or **scaffolding** in effective instruction, as well as the importance of prosody in skilled reading. As was seen in the example from *Alice in Wonderland* earlier in this chapter, when children's phrasing of text fails to follow the general flow of oral language, comprehension can suffer. By helping students recognize where appropriate breaks fall within a text, you are helping them see how attributes of oral language can and should be applied to written language. This can be done either indirectly, through the modeling of phrase breaks in your oral reading, or directly, by demonstrating to students exactly where those breaks lie within a written text.

The strategies that I discuss throughout this book incorporate these four crucial principles and are designed to help you integrate effective oral reading instruction into your literacy lessons. As such, they substantially increase the likelihood that all your students will become fluent readers.

Fluency Approaches to Support the Reading of Challenging Text in Multiple Settings

Three approaches to fluency instruction—echo, choral, and partner reading—can be implemented easily in a variety of grouping formats and can be used to support the reading of a range of challenging texts across a range of grade levels.

Echo Reading

The first of these fluency strategies is **echo reading**. It is a teacher-assisted approach to oral reading and provides the most scaffolding of the three strategies that comprise this section. As with all three strategies, the procedure is very simple. It involves your reading of a section of a text aloud while your students follow along in their own copy. Once you have completed a section, your children read back the same text to you as a group. This strategy offers your learners a great deal of modeling and a considerable amount of support. In fact, this simple procedure provides your children with a model of accurate word reading, phrasing, pacing, and use of expression. You can also adjust the amount of text that your students read at one time depending on the text's difficulty; in other words, you can read longer sections of text when your selection is easier and shorter sections of material when the passage is more challenging. It can also be used with texts from your literacy curriculum or from your content-area instruction.

Because echo reading provides your students with considerable scaffolding, it is an approach that should not be used with text at your students' independent levels. Similarly, text that is at your students' instructional level is unlikely to need the amount of support this procedure provides. Instead, I recommend echo reading for texts that are considered to be *challenging*. Since this procedure can be used whenever you encounter difficult text, you may find it effective to teach your students the process early in the school year so that they know what is expected of them. Then you can revert to it whenever they need support for a challenging selection.

Lesson Snapshot

Despite the ease with which echo reading is conducted, certain elements are critical to its success:

- First, each student must have a copy of the text. Next, all your students need to know where you are beginning your reading so they can follow along from the correct point in their text. You can also ask them to track the material as you read to them to help them stay engaged. If you choose to, you can read the text to them in its entirety and discuss the selection prior to beginning the echo reading procedure. This will allow them to develop a sense of the text as a whole. If you decide to do this, have them follow along with your initial reading of the material as well.

- Second, it is important that your children understand the process they are about to engage in. Explain to them that their role is to listen and follow along when it is your turn to read, and to read aloud themselves, as a group, when it is their turn. During this procedure, consider walking around the room in order to ensure that students are keeping up with your reading and are actively engaged in reading back each section when it is their turn.

- Third, it is important that you build up the amount of reading that the children complete at one time. At first, it is likely that they will have difficulty echoing what you have just read to them, and it may take a while for them to get used to the process. However, because you do not want them relying on their auditory memory to respond correctly, it is essential that you increase the amount of text that they echo while reading. In order to assist them with this process, you may want to start by reading a sentence or two, but you should gradually build up to several paragraphs—or even a page—of text at a time, depending on your students' age, ability, and the amount of material on each page.

Choral Reading

The next teacher-assisted instructional approach is **choral reading**.
While choral reading provides students with less scaffolding than
echo reading, it still presents learners with a model for developing both their automaticity and their prosody. In this approach, the
teacher and students simultaneously read a text or a section of a text
aloud. Since you and your students are reading a selection at the
same time, I recommend that you proceed in one of two ways. First,
you could use it as a follow-up approach to the echo reading of a
challenging text, providing the learners with an extra guided reading of the material; should you use it in this manner, you will be
following a gradual release of responsibility model, such as is
presented in Fluency-Oriented Reading Instruction and Wide
Fluency-Oriented Reading Instruction approaches (see Chapter 3).

Alternatively, choral reading can be used with a text that is at
the beginning of your students' instructional level; that is, material
that requires a minimal amount of scaffolding before the students
can work with it independently. For example, your students may be
able to decode most of the words in a given selection, but need to
work on their reading rate, or you may be working with a piece that
calls for expression, such as a poem, a speech, or highly descriptive
passages, provided they are not too long or too difficult. By reading
such selections with your learners, you may find that their reading
becomes more fluent not only when they are reading along with you
but also when they next attempt to read the material on their own.
Although choral reading does not provide the same degree of support that you find with echo reading, it is an enjoyable approach to
fluency development and one that has an important role in bringing
text alive.

Lesson Snapshot

Choral reading is another straightforward approach, but students must be comfortable with the procedure if they are to benefit from its use in the curriculum:

- As with any of the fluency-oriented approaches, each of your students must have her own copy of the material you will be reading together. Be aware that when you are first introducing the approach, you may need to help your students locate where you are starting your reading. You likely will need to circulate around the room to ensure they are following along in their texts.

- Just as with echo reading, you will need to explain the process to your students. They should understand that they are going to be reading in unison with you and that you are going to be emphasizing the appropriate pace and use of expression with them—and that it is their job to try to mimic you! Eventually, as they feel more comfortable with their reading of a particular text, they may want to develop their own interpretation, but for now they should try to read as a group.

- It is also important to build up the amount of text that your students can choral read with you. In order to do this, you may want to begin with short poems or passages from a longer text. Then, as students develop familiarity with the process, you can quickly build up to lengthier selections. However, you may want to continue circulating around the room to ensure that all the students are actively participating in the reading—with their eyes on the text—rather than simply repeating what they hear being said.

- Once the students are comfortable with this procedure, you can create variations. For example, you can select poems for two voices and ask the students to choral read based on:
  - their rows, tables, or by dividing the room into halves
  - their first or last initials (A through L versus M through Z)
  - counting off as ones or twos
  - any other division you can think of that is good-natured and that the kids will enjoy.

Partner Reading

The final supplemental approach is that of **partner reading**. This is also a very simple yet effective strategy for developing reading fluency. As with echo and choral reading, partner reading significantly increases the amount of reading that students complete in a given period; however, it is not a teacher-assisted approach. Instead, students work in pairs to provide one another with support in the oral reading of a selection. The children take turns—with one child reading approximately a page of text aloud while the child's partner follows along, listening and providing support and assistance. This support can consist of sounding out words, providing unknown words, and correcting misread words. The listener can also ask his partner if a word makes sense in a sentence, provide positive feedback or encouragement, or help the reader keep track of the reading. You may want to promote the use of these forms of assistance by modeling them for your students both in your own instruction and in demonstrations you conduct for your learners.

Of the three strategies discussed here, partner reading provides the least amount of scaffolding. As such, it should be used either to practice rereading a more challenging selection, perhaps one the students have previously echo or choral read with their teacher, or to read a text that is closer to the students' independent reading level. In partner reading, students alternate reading every other page throughout an entire selection. This allows the learners to read significant amounts of text with support from their partner. Rather than reading slightly over one minute for every thirty minutes of class time in round-robin reading, these students are each reading fifteen minutes during the same period of time. This simple shift in oral reading strategies allows students to increase their reading time by a factor of fifteen—a pretty powerful way of increasing their engagement with text! Although partner reading does not provide the learners with the same level of scaffolding as echo or choral reading, it is an effective way of ensuring that your students are spending significant amounts of time reading connected text in a supportive environment. And, because they provide students with support and extensive opportunities to read connected text, echo, choral, and partner reading are all effective aids to your students' overall reading development.

Lesson Snapshot

Since partner reading requires the students to read a given text themselves, it is important that you present them with a clear understanding of the procedure:

- Before beginning partner reading, discuss the roles both students have in the process. First, the students each take turns reading and listening to one another read. Second, the listener should follow along in the text, paying attention to what the reader is reading. Third, the listener should also provide help and encouragement whenever the reader has difficulties with the text. As always, it is important that students have their own copies of the text, both to read from and to follow along in as their partners read.

- You can select partners for your students or they can self-select their pairs. If you are selecting pairs, the best method involves pairing readers across reading ability levels. But you do not want the differences between the learners to be so great that the partners get frustrated. The easiest way to accomplish this is by making two lists in which you place your most skilled reader at the top of the first list and the student who is experiencing the most difficulty with their reading development at the bottom of the second list. You should place your next most skilled reader on the first list and your reader who is having somewhat less difficulty on the second list. Continue with this process, working your way through your class, until every student is listed. Place

continued

the two groups side by side and match across the two lists. This should match your most skilled reader with a student who is an average reader and the student who is experiencing the greatest difficulty with a student who is also an average reader. Such pairings should increase the effectiveness of the process since the differences between the readers are substantial enough to maximize your learners' growth.

- Your role in this process is to circulate around the room, not only to help keep the students focused, but also to provide the partners with assistance as they need it.

- Until the learners become comfortable with the partner reading process, they should read short passages, say a paragraph or two, before switching off with their partner. As they develop stamina, readers can extend the amount of text they are reading, until they are able to cover about a page each (taking care to complete any sentence or paragraph that continues onto the next page).

- Should there be time available after reading through the selection once, students can complete a second reading with their partners; however, during their second turn, the partners should read the pages opposite to those they read initially (i.e., reading the odd pages if they read the even pages the first time through and the even pages if they initially read the odd pages).

This chapter provides you with a snapshot of fluency's role in the reading process and our education system, along with several principles and basic approaches for integrating effective fluency instruction into your classroom. The rest of the book will present a range of methods for use in specific classroom situations. I am certain you will find an instructional intervention that will work for you and your students, one that will enable you to integrate effective fluency instruction into your classroom and will assist your learners in their development as they become skilled, independent readers.

- Do you envision integrating fluency instruction into your reading curriculum? If so, where do you feel there is a natural fit?

- Do you feel your students' reading development has followed the stages outlined at the beginning of the chapter? If so, do you feel they are on a trajectory to become skilled readers? If not, what instructional focus might assist them with their reading development?

- Why is it important that students' word recognition becomes automatic as well as accurate? Similarly, why is it important that students develop the ability to use appropriate phrasing and expression?

- Pick a chapter from the latter part of this book—or another book that you and your colleagues have not previously read—and go around the group reading aloud a paragraph each. What did you do and how did the process make you feel? Thinking back, both on your own experience with round-robin reading and the discussion in this chapter, what are some of the problems students' experience with the process? Given all the negatives associated with the approach, why do you think its use persists in many classrooms?

- How do you think the four principles outlined in the final section of the chapter help to support effective fluency instruction?

- Can you think of situations in which echo, choral, or partner reading could replace the oral reading instruction you are currently using in your literacy curriculum?

Notes

1. All teacher and student names are pseudonyms.

2. While decoding instruction—and other word recognition instruction—is necessary if learners are to become fluent readers, it is beyond the focus of this book. Instead, the instructional approaches included here assume that learners have established some degree of decoding ability and concentrate on the development of automaticity and the incorporation of elements such as appropriate expression and phrasing.

3. Since the preponderance of words used in early reading material fall within students' oral vocabulary, once students have correctly identified a word, they are likely to know its meaning. This balance begins to shift as texts become more complex and the number of words that are decodable, but outside students' oral vocabulary, increases.

4. Clearly comprehension is multifaceted and much broader than word recognition, however, at this point in the discussion, I am focusing on the contribution automatic decoding makes to skilled reading.

Chapter 2

Evaluating Fluent Reading

■ Why is fluency assessment important?

■ How can you evaluate your students' reading rate and their use of prosody?

■ How can you determine appropriate reading levels (independent, instructional, and frustration) for your students?

Assessing Reading Fluency— The Hows and the Whys

So you want to use a whole-class fluency approach with your second or third graders and need to demonstrate their growth over the course of a marking period or the school year. Or you think fluency instruction might be something you should integrate into your literacy curriculum, but need to identify which of your students would benefit from this instruction. Luckily, several measures are available that can help inform your fluency instruction by providing you with authentic assessments of your students' oral reading.

It is important to conduct fluency assessments with texts that you are using for your literacy instruction for a number of reasons

(McKenna & Stahl, 2003; Kuhn, 2007). First, assessments allow you to determine how fluent your students are on **grade-level texts**, or texts written for a particular age group. Since most content-area materials are written at grade level or higher, determining this will help you gauge the amount of support your learners will need to read these texts successfully. Second, assessments allow you to identify your students' independent, instructional, and frustration levels, which is critical to text selection both for instruction and for independent reading. Third, by conducting oral reading assessments at the beginning of the year and at set points throughout the year, you can track student gains, both individually and as a class, in terms of their correct words per minute rate, the most concrete fluency measure, and in terms of expression and phrasing, aspects of fluency that, while less quantifiable than **reading rate** and accuracy, are just as crucial to their reading development. Ultimately, these assessments will help you see whether the reading approaches you are using are effective at developing your learners' fluency, whether any of your students would benefit from fluency-oriented instruction, and what your instructional goals for these learners should be.

Evaluating Accurate and Automatic Word Recognition

Although there are multiple ways of evaluating your students' reading fluency, it is probably easiest to begin with the most concrete measure: the number of **correct words per minute (cwpm)**. This figure actually combines two components of a reader's fluency: *accuracy*, or the number of words a reader is able to correctly identify in a text, and *automaticity*, or the rate at which a learner reads a given text. Because of the ease with which you can determine this figure, cwpm is also the most commonly used fluency measure and the one you are most likely to be familiar with. In fact, it is often the only measure of students' reading fluency—a tendency that can be problematic because it leads learners to view fluency as fast reading—clearly only part of the picture! I cannot stress enough the importance of considering all aspects of fluency in your evaluations—and your instruction.

The basic principle behind the cwpm measure is quite straightforward: listen to a student read an unpracticed text in order to determine the number of words they read per minute as well as how many of those words are read correctly. You can choose to conduct this reading in one of several ways as long as your students perform a cold reading of the text. In other words, you should not assess your students' fluency on texts they have already read because even a small amount of practice is likely to affect how well they read a given selection. While this runs contrary to the advice I give throughout the remainder of this book—that individual students should not be asked to read aloud from an unpracticed text—I want to stress that evaluating your students' reading is an exception to this rule.

Selecting Appropriate Reading Material

Let's look at your options regarding the range of reading material first. You can ask your students to read either from a text that you are using as part of the classroom literacy curriculum or from a text that has been devised specifically for assessment purposes. For example, if you are reading from a literature anthology or basal reader, simply select the next passage and ask your students to read it aloud, noting the number of **miscues** (responses that differ from a written word) and how many words they are able to read in a one-minute period. Since your students probably work on a daily basis with this material, the cwpm assessment will provide you with valuable information. Do not assume, though, that all the stories in a collection are on grade level. Some selections will be written below

grade level and some will be written above. This does not negate
the value of using these materials, but it is an important point to
bear in mind.

If you are using guided reading groups, you could select the
next book in a series for the assessment. Keep in mind, however,
that series books are designed to be at the child's instructional level,
and your learner's cwpm rating will reflect this (that is, they might
read their guided reading books more fluently than they would
grade-level texts). Remember, too, at least in the primary grades,
that students are usually more familiar with **narrative texts**, which
tell a story, than they are with **expository texts**, which provide information. If you ask them, for instance, to read from a science-based
trade book or social science text book, their reading might be negatively affected. Given all these possible options, your best bets may
be a grade-level narrative text, a guided reading text, and a selection
from your content-area material (if you do not use these types of
materials, make your selection from among those you do use). You
can still use these materials for instruction, but wait until after the
students have been evaluated on them. Since each reading is only
a minute long, you should be able to conduct all three readings in
about five minutes per student, and each evaluation will provide
you with a different yet vital piece of information. If you have
students who are clearly reading below grade level, reading from
grade-level texts will not yield any useful information for you and
will only serve to frustrate or demoralize them. Instead, ask these
students to read exclusively from instructional-level texts.

An alternative to using classroom-based texts is to select material designed for reading assessments. For example, you could use
an **Informal Reading Inventory (IRI)**. A number of these are available on the market and are useful for a range of evaluations, from
word identification in isolation to comprehension. Since you probably have a sense of where your particular students are reading,

you can start off by asking them to read a passage that you consider to be at their independent or instructional level, then proceed to a grade-level passage or until they reach frustration on a given selection (each IRI provides guidelines regarding what constitutes independent, instructional, and frustration levels for a reader on a given passage). Most IRIs also have several selections at each level so you can evaluate your students at different time points over the course of the year without making them reread the same passage. Similarly, the inventories usually have narrative and expository selections so you can gain insight into your students' comfort levels both with stories and with content-area texts. IRIs allow you to evaluate your students' reading across a range of levels (both instructional and grade) and genres (narrative and expository).

Determining Students' CWPM Rate

Determining your students' cwpm rate traditionally entails selecting a text that you have previously identified for assessment and asking your students to read aloud for one minute, starting at the beginning. If you are conducting a number of evaluations at once, you may want to mark off a one-hundred- to two-hundred-word passage (depending on students' age and reading ability). This will allow you to more easily estimate your students' reading rate. You should also make a copy of any text you will be using (one for each student), so that you can note the learner's name, any miscues, and how far she was able to read in one minute directly onto the duplicate. Then you can determine their exact cwpm rating at a later time.

If you feel that this one-minute sample does not provide you with adequate information about your students, you can ask them to read out loud for several minutes prior to beginning your evaluation. This gives them a chance to warm up (Valencia et al., 2005) and you a more accurate sense of their reading fluency. You may want to try this with several students to see if it makes a noticeable difference to their reading. Alternatively, you could take several one-minute samples from the text (I suggest three) and average the student's ratings across the passages. If you choose this option, make sure that all your passages are selected either from the same text or, if that is not possible because of the text's length, from texts that are equivalently leveled to maximize the ratings' reliability—not always an easy task given the qualitative differences between books. If, on the other hand, your selection is relatively lengthy, you could have your students read continuously for three minutes and simply divide your total by three.

The next step involves comparing your students' cwpm rate against an established norm to determine whether they are making reasonable progress in terms of accuracy and automaticity. Fortunately, several excellent tables are available that provide a range of cwpm averages at several time points (usually fall, winter, and spring) across a given grade level as well as across a range of grades (usually first through eighth; Hasbrouck & Tindal, 1992; Rasinski, 2003). The cwpm norms presented in Table 2.1 offer one example, adapted by Tim Rasinski (2004) for Pacific Resources for Education and Learning (PREL).

When comparing your students' cwpm rates with the norms established for PREL, there are two points to bear in mind. First, the norms outlined in this table represent an average range. If you have only a few learners whose reading rate is significantly below this average, it is likely that the majority of your class are making suitable progress, and either one-on-one or small-group fluency instruction would be more appropriate for those students who would benefit from this work. You can find such strategies in Chapters 4 or 5 (for example, the Oral Recitation Lesson [Hoffman, 1987]; reading-while-listening [Chomsky, 1976]; or repeated readings [Samuels, 1979]). On the other hand, if the majority of your students fall below these guidelines, then it is likely that your class would benefit from either

Table 2.1

Correct Words Per Minute (CWPM) by Grade Level

Grade	Fall	Winter	Spring
1	—	10–30	30–60
2	30–60	50–80	70–100
3	50–90	70–100	80–110
4	70–110	80–120	100–140
5	80–120	100–140	110–150
6	100–140	110–150	120–160
7	110–150	120–160	130–170
8	120–160	130–170	140–180

Source: Rasinski, T. V. (2004). *Assessing Reading Fluency*. Honolulu: Pacific Resources for Education and Learning. Available at www.prel.org/products/re_/assessing-fluency.htm.

shared reading approaches (Chapter 3) or supplemental approaches that can be woven into your literacy curriculum (Chapter 6) as the basis of your fluency instruction (for example, Wide Fluency-Oriented Reading Instruction [Kuhn et al., 2006]; the Fluency Development Lesson [Rasinski et al., 1994]; or paired repeated reading [Koskinen & Blum, 1984, 1986]).

The second point involves what I refer to as the **summer slump**; that is, students often lose some of the gains they made over the course of the school year during their summer vacation (Allington, 2005), and this is reflected in the PREL norms. For example, if you look at the spring cwpm norms for fourth grade (100–140 cwpm), you will notice that the range is higher than that listed for the fall of fifth grade (80–120 cwpm). This occurs quite consistently throughout the table. While not necessarily surprising, it highlights the value of encouraging your students to read over the summer to counter some of these losses. This is especially important for students from lower socioeconomic status (SES) communities for whom the achievement gap grows with each passing year. While students across the economic strata make similar gains over the course of the school year, students at schools serving lower SES communities experience greater losses over the summer than do their peers at schools serving higher SES communities (Allington, 2005). This puts students in lower SES communities at a significant disadvantage; over the course of each school year just to stay even, they would not only have to make gains in learning equivalent to their peers in higher SES communities but would also have to make up for the additional losses they experienced over the summer.

Given that you can't be with your students outside the school year (or even the school day), the best way to help them minimize these losses is to encourage them to become engaged readers. Since skilled readers are more likely to engage with texts than are struggling readers, they are more likely to read on their own over the summer and less likely to experience as significant a loss (Anderson, Wilson, & Fielding, 1988; Stanovich, 1986). By helping your students become fluent readers, it is likely that you will also help them with their overall academic achievement.

Evaluating Prosodic Reading

Although it is important to determine how well students' reading rate and accuracy are progressing, it is equally important to evaluate the elements of their reading that, taken together, make up expression or *prosody*. The recently increased emphasis—or overemphasis—on improving the number of correct words that learners are able to read in a minute (e.g. Walker, Mokhtari, & Sargent, 2006) has led in some cases to a skewed understanding of what we expect from our developing readers, who may develop the notion that good reading is fast reading, and the faster the better. Instead, students should be developing the understanding that good oral reading sounds like language,[1] with appropriate phrasing, stress, emphasis, *and* pace (a point you can easily demonstrate by racing through a passage aloud to indicate how awkward it sounds). Because prosodic elements are less concrete than rate and accuracy, they are more open to interpretation on the part of the listener than a cwpm rating. Nevertheless, a number of excellent reading scales take these aspects of fluent reading into account (e.g., Allington, 1983; Zutell and Rasinksi, 1991; the National Assessment of Educational Progress [NAEP], 1995).

The scale that is perhaps easiest to use is the National Assessment of Educational Progress (NAEP) Oral Reading Fluency Scale (National Center for Education Statistics, 1995) (see Table 2.2). It uses four levels of description to evaluate students' oral reading ability. The NAEP itself is a national evaluation of the academic achievement of the country's fourth, eighth, and twelfth graders (McKenna & Stahl, 2003). As such, it looks at a variety of academic measures, including reading fluency. The fluency scale of the NAEP looks at the degree to which students' reading incorporates prosodic elements of pace, smoothness, phrasing, and expression. The four levels of the scale range from reading that is primarily word by word and lacking in expression (the most basic level) to reading that is expressive and incorporates appropriate phrasing and pace (the highest level). Beginning readers will likely be reading at level 1 and, ideally, older students (in grades four and beyond) will be reading at level 4, at least on grade-level texts. Keep in mind that since you will be making judgment calls regarding which level best represents the prosodic components of your learners' reading

Table 2.2

National Assessment of Educational Progress: Oral Reading Fluency Scale

Level 4	Reads primarily in larger, meaningful phrase groups. Although some regressions, repetitions, and deviations from text may be present, these do not appear to detract from the overall structure of the story. Preservation of the author's syntax is consistent. Some or most of the story is read with expressive interpretation.
Level 3	Reads primarily in three- or four-word phrase groups. Some small groupings may be present. However, the majority of phrasing seems appropriate and preserves the syntax of the author. Little or no expressive interpretation is present.
Level 2	Reads primarily in two-word phrases with some three- or four-word groupings. Some word-by-word reading may be present. Word groupings may seem awkward and unrelated to larger context of sentence or passage.
Level 1	Reads primarily word-by-word. Occasional two-word or three-word phrases may occur, but these are infrequent and/or they do not preserve meaningful syntax.

fluency, there may be some variability between your evaluation and that of other assessors. This can best be remedied by working with your fellow teachers to discuss your ratings and coming to some level of consensus. Overall, these categories are broad enough that there should be general agreement regarding which of the four levels best characterize each of your students' oral reading. I have found that this scale lends itself to a higher percentage of initial agreement between myself and other listeners than other scales mentioned—in some cases, as high as 100 percent!

In terms of development, expect that your first graders will be reading in a word-by-word manner throughout most of the year

(NAEP level 1). At the end of first grade and beginning of the second, you should see a shift to two-word phrases, although it is still unlikely that they will be able to read with a great deal of expression (NAEP level 2). Since second and third grade are considered to be periods during which learners consolidate their word knowledge and begin to incorporate expression and appropriate phrasing into their reading, they should move through NAEP level 3 and possibly even into NAEP level 4 during this time frame. Ideally, by grade 4 and beyond, your readers will have reached NAEP level 4 on most grade-level texts. As with the cwpm guidelines discussed earlier, some of your students will achieve these levels sooner than others. If, on the other hand, you have students who seem to be having difficulty making the transition to the type of phrasing and expression you normally hear in skilled oral reading—that is, if the students' reading sounds stilted or they are racing through the text—you may want to provide additional fluency-oriented instruction for them. This could be simply integrating a focus on Tim Rasinski's (2003) fluency principles (expression, modeling, phrasing, and the provision of support; see Chapter 1 for a discussion of these principles) into your literacy instruction, or it may involve adopting a more directed instructional approach such as those outlined throughout this book to help your students' oral reading become fluid and expressive.

Because fluent reading is multidimensional, the use of the NAEP scale (or one of the other available scales) in tandem with a cwpm table will give you a fuller picture of your students' fluency development than does the use of a cwpm table alone. This combination also better allows you to pinpoint whether your students need targeted fluency instruction and, if they do, whether it should focus on fluency broadly (accuracy, automaticity, and prosody) or on specific aspects of the construct. Since both evaluations can be conducted on the same selection and completed relatively quickly, it makes sense to use them together as your students read orally from a designated text. However, consider tape-recording their oral reading to help you with the accuracy of your evaluations. This will allow you to confirm the cwpm rate for each student and, if needed, to listen to their use of phrasing and expression multiple times to confirm your ranking of their prosodic features.

Identifying Students' Reading Levels

A final reason to evaluate your students' accuracy is to help you identify their independent, instructional, and frustration reading levels. To determine these levels, begin with the percentages of correct words that are generally accepted for each (Betts, 1946; Leslie & Caldwell, 1995)[2]: 98 percent or higher for an **independent reading level text**; 95 to 97 percent for an **instructional reading level text**; and below 95 percent for a **frustration level text**. While these are useful as a baseline, it is worthwhile to incorporate rate and prosody into this understanding as well. For example, you may find that, although your students are able to read a text with a high degree of accuracy, they are extremely slow or, alternatively, are able to read at a reasonable rate and with relatively few miscues but have inappropriate phrasing. Further, you can gain valuable insight into a learner's comfort with a selection simply by asking them what the passage was about once they finish reading it. If a student has no sense of what the passage was about despite sounding fluent, that text is unlikely to be a good choice for their independent reading but may be appropriate for comprehension instruction. On the other hand, some students may read the selection relatively slowly but with a high degree of comprehension, and could benefit from texts at that level. Interest can also be a factor in this evaluation process. A student who has a lot of interest in a subject may be willing and able to read a text that would otherwise be too difficult, as the recent Harry Potter phenomenon attests. When looking at the approaches in this book, it will become clear that the range for instructional level texts can be expanded if sufficient support is provided for the readers. Taken together, the factors mentioned here can help you determine how best to use a particular text both for specific children and within your literacy curriculum in general. However, it is always important to remember that these are guidelines and, as such, you should be flexible regarding which texts you select for a given situation.

Three Points Worth Revisiting— Conducting Valid Fluency Assessments

Before leaving the topic of assessment, three considerations are worthy of reiteration. First, when you conduct these assessments, it is essential that your students read from a text they have not previously practiced; in other words, the evaluation should be a cold reading on a new selection. Even a small amount of practice can affect how well your students read a particular text, and you will be unlikely to get an accurate picture of your students' oral reading. Second, record your students' oral reading. While you are likely to get a fairly reliable analysis just by listening, recording your students enables you to confirm their words-per-minute rate, miscues, and prosody ratings. Even though I have been conducting evaluations of struggling readers for over twenty years, I still record the reading of every student I work with and use it to reconfirm my analysis of their oral reading. Since each student is reading aloud for only a few minutes, you will probably need no more than one or two audiotapes; if you use a digital recorder, it probably will not be an issue. Given the ease with which you can misunderstand what has been read, such recordings increase the likelihood that you have established a reliable evaluation of your students' reading fluency.

The third consideration concerns the importance of assessing your students both on instructional level text *and* on grade-level material to the degree possible. While it is essential that your learners spend part of their school day working with selections at their instructional level—and you need to know what constitutes an instructional level text for each of your students—it is also critical that you have a sense of how well they are able to handle grade-level material. Since much of the content area and shared reading that they will be undertaking uses selections that are at, or even above, grade level, it is necessary that you understand how much support your readers will need in order to be successful with this material. And, since an increasing amount of weight is being placed on standardized assessments designed to measure students' success with grade-level texts, to ignore this facet of their reading ability would be to do a disservice to them. By evaluating students on grade-level material, you will develop a clearer understanding of their reading abilities and the types of support they will need in order to succeed with that material. While such an evaluation provides useful insight into your learners' reading ability, the goal is not to set your students up for failure. If you are teaching fifth graders, for example, and you have a student who is reading second-grade texts at an instructional level, it is unlikely that the student will be successful with fifth-grade material. Instead, you may want to see how well they are able to read a third- or fourth-grade passage. Students who experience success with these selections and do not feel frustrated can continue with fifth-grade material. If, on the other hand, these readers are barely able to read through the passages at the earlier grade levels (i.e., the number of miscues is high, their reading is extremely slow, or they have little comprehension), then it is reasonable to stop at one of the passages at an earlier grade level (e.g., third or fourth). Whatever the format you decide on for evaluating your learners' oral reading, it will provide you with valuable insight into their fluency development and their potential need for fluency-oriented instruction.

Study Guide Questions

- Why is it important that you assess your students' reading fluency? How should word recognition be evaluated? How can the more global elements of fluency (e.g., expression, phrasing) be evaluated?

- Create tapes of several learners reading for one-minute periods (ideally a struggling, average, and very fluent reader). Pair up with another teacher and compare your evaluations of these students in terms of both the correct words per minute scale and the NAEP fluency scale.

- How can you identify your students' independent, instructional and frustration reading levels? What factors can mediate these levels, allowing students to use more challenging texts?

- Why is it important to evaluate your students on a passage they have not read previously?

- Why is it useful to evaluate students on both instructional level material (e.g., their guided reading texts) and grade-level material (e.g., their shared reading text or a content-area text) whenever possible?

Notes

1. Since there are clearly a number of literary devices used in written text that do not appear in oral language, oral reading is not an exact equivalent of speech; however, the use of this phrase helps students recognize the link between the two and is shorthand for the type of expressive or prosodic reading that you want them to engage in.

2. These are the percentages that Lauren Leslie and JoAnne Caldwell use for counting miscues they consider to be meaning changing (e.g., insertions, omissions, substitutions).

Chapter 3

Fluency Development and Whole-Class Instruction
Approaches for Shared Reading

With Paula Schwanenflugel

Instructional Approach	Grade Levels	Grouping	Type of Text
FORI (Fluency-Oriented Reading Instruction)	• Originally grade 2 • Can be used with grades 3 and above (primarily in small groups)	• Originally whole class • Can be used with small groups	Longer, challenging texts (twenty to forty minutes of reading per day)
Wide Reading	• Originally grade 2 • Can be used with grades 3 and above (primarily in small groups)	• Originally whole class • Can be used with small groups	Longer, challenging texts (twenty to forty minutes of reading per day)

■ What roles do repeated reading and wide reading play in fluency development?

■ What approaches can you use for shared repeated reading?

■ How can you integrate multiple texts into shared reading?

Whole-Class Approaches to Fluency Instruction

While it is easy to say that round-robin reading is an ineffective approach to oral reading instruction (e.g., Rasinski, 2006), until recently, it was difficult for teachers to find an effective alternative for whole-class instruction. Since the mid-nineties, two approaches have emerged that have been successfully used as part of the **shared reading** component of the literacy curriculum. The first of these, Fluency-Oriented Reading Instruction (FORI; Stahl & Heubach, 2005) incorporates the use of repetition, and the second, Wide Fluency-Oriented Reading Instruction (Wide FORI; Kuhn et al., 2006), makes use of multiple texts coupled with **scaffolded reading strategies**. These two approaches are designed for whole-class instruction and are meant for second and third graders—students who are making the transition to fluent reading at what we consider to be a developmentally appropriate point. That said, both could easily be modified for use with smaller groups of older struggling readers (i.e., grades four and above). Underlying both approaches are concepts presented as part of the Oral Recitation Lesson (Hoffman, 1987; see Chapter 4 for a discussion of the Oral Recitation Lesson), such as a focus on comprehension early in the weekly lesson plan and the modeling of the expressive elements of a text. Prior to addressing these approaches, we feel it is important to discuss the role that both repetition and the scaffolded reading of a wide range of texts can play in the development of your students' reading fluency.

Repetition Versus Scaffolded Wide Reading

For years, one of the basic tenets of fluency instruction has been repetition. In a seminal article about both automaticity theory and fluency instruction, "The Method of Repeated Readings," Jay Samuels (1979) argues that students who are experiencing difficulties developing automatic word recognition might benefit from seeing a given text multiple times. He bases his argument on the fact that, in the majority of classrooms, then and now, students are exposed to a given text only once before moving on to new material. He suggests it might be useful to have students reread a given text several times. Such rereadings would enable learners to develop familiarity with a given piece to the point where they could read it automatically. Significantly, over the past three decades this approach has proven effective in developing the reading rate and accuracy of many students. As a result, repetition has become an underlying principle in a host of successful instructional methods designed to increase learners' fluency (e.g., Dowhower, 1989; National Reading Panel, 2000).

However, in a recent review of fluency instruction (Kuhn & Stahl, 2003), my colleague Steven Stahl and I noticed that when comparing approaches based on repetition with those that incorporate *scaffolded* reading of an equivalent amount of different texts, both methods of instruction appeared to lead to equivalent gains. This led us to wonder: is there something unique in the repetition of texts that leads to increased reading fluency or is it possible that the reading of challenging texts for sufficient amounts of time (e.g., a minimum of twenty to thirty minutes per day) with adequate support can lead to similar results? A number of studies conducted in the years since this review was published have indicated that, not only is supported wide reading as effective as repeated reading in developing critical components of fluency such as accurate and automatic word recognition, text comprehension, and prosody, but it may be more effective (e.g., Kuhn, 2005; Kuhn et al., 2006; Mostow & Beck, 2005; Schwebel, 2007). This may be because it is easier to learn a given word when you see it in a variety of contexts than if you see it in the same context multiple times. For example, students are likely to learn a word, say, the word *sun*, more quickly if they see it in three different contexts (the *sun* sets, the yellow *sun*, and the *sun* and stars) than if they see the same context (the *sun* sets) three times (Mostow & Beck, 2005). Given the overlap of words that exist in texts at all levels, but especially in the early elementary grades, it seems likely that by providing students with access to many supported texts, you are increasing the chances that they will encounter words in just such multiple contexts.

Appropriate Texts, Appropriate Settings

Clearly, students need significant amounts of practice reading connected text in order to become fluent, but there are two important caveats (Kuhn et al., 2006). The first involves the type of text you use and the second involves the types of instructional settings that are appropriate. We feel it is essential that you use **challenging text** as the basis of your fluency instruction. This means having students read material considered to be at the top end of their instructional level or even the beginning of their frustration level (i.e., 85% to 90% accuracy on the initial reading). While we would not normally expect students to work with challenging texts even in instructional settings, students experience tremendous success with such material *provided they have sufficient support*. In fact, virtually all the approaches in this book use material that many educators would consider too difficult for learners if they were taking part in a typical reading lesson; yet, because these methods are carefully scaffolded, they are successful. In the FORI program, Steven Stahl and Kathleen Heubach found that students experienced success with just such texts. And in our own use of challenging text (Kuhn & Schwanenflugel, 2006), we found that, over the course of a week, students were able to go from the twenty-fifth to the seventy-fifth percentile in terms of their cwpm rate based on the norms determined by Jan Hasbrouck and Gerald Tindal (1992). On the other hand, when learners read texts with which they are already fairly fluent, scaffolding results in relatively little gain, if any at all (e.g., Hollingsworth, 1970). This makes sense, since there is little room for growth when students use such texts. These results suggest that you use challenging material for fluency instruction, even if it is too difficult for other literacy activities such as guided reading.

The second caveat concerns the instructional setting in which your students read challenging material. We have already alluded to this issue, but it is important to remember that when we refer to wide reading, we are not talking about an independent reading period such as Drop Everything and Read (DEAR) time or Sustained Silent Reading (SSR). Rather, we are discussing a carefully structured and supported approach to the reading of multiple texts as part of your shared reading instruction. If you do have an independent reading period, we also encourage you to provide your learners with the *option* of using supported reading approaches during this time. Rather than simply asking students to read independently, we feel students can benefit from having several strategies available during this time, including partner reading; *mumble reading* (reading performed so quietly it sounds like mumbling to a passerby); the use of "phones" made from PVC pipes to direct children's voices back to themselves; and the inclusion of books on tape, CDs, or podcasts. We have found that the students who are most in need of additional practice are also the students most likely to take part in avoidance activities when it comes to reading on their own (e.g., Hasbrouck, 2006). Drawing attention to their dilemma by providing these options only to your struggling readers does little to develop their confidence. By instead opening up these alternatives to all your students, your struggling readers can receive the practice they need without singling them out.

Fluency-Oriented Reading Instruction (FORI)

The first strategy, Fluency-Oriented Reading Instruction (FORI; Stahl & Heubach, 2005), was designed for whole-class instruction. It was developed in response to a districtwide mandate that required schools to use only grade-level material for their reading lessons—despite a wide range of reading levels in the district's classrooms. In fact, because the district served many low-SES households, there was a real concern that grade-level texts would be well above the instructional level for the majority of the children and would set them up for failure. In response, both the teachers and the researchers decided to create a program they hoped would maximize the students' chances of success. They hoped that, by incorporating extensive amounts of support or scaffolding as part of the overall lesson plan, the learners would benefit from instruction within the classroom.

Stahl and Heubach worked with the teachers to create an intervention that would support the learners' reading development. Their program was both straightforward and based on significant amounts of scaffolded practice. One of the primary program goals was the provision of heavily scaffolded reading instruction to ensure that students have multiple opportunities to read each selection. The schools that first worked with the approach built their lesson plans around selections from the **basal reader** that were part of their literacy curriculum. Since then, however, teachers have experienced equal success using both *trade books* and **literature anthologies**. Should you decide to use FORI with either basal readers or literature anthologies, it is critical that you select collections designed for your class's grade level. On the other hand, if you are working with trade books, we suggest employing a system that evaluates the reading levels for individual selections; for example, see Fountas and Pinnell (1999) or Gunning (1997), to help you select grade-level texts.

The FORI approach proved successful with the students in the initial study (Stahl & Heubach, 2005), with children making an average growth of 1.8 years in the first year of the intervention and 1.7 years in the second year on the Qualitative Reading Inventory (QRI; Leslie & Caldwell, 1995). FORI is a five-day program that is relatively easy to implement. However, if you decide to use this program, it is essential that the students read connected text for at least twenty to thirty minutes per day. So, for example, if you are using poems or other short selections, your learners will not be spending sufficient time engaged with print for their word recognition to become automatic. It is, therefore, critical that you find alternatives, such as older anthologies that your school may have kept from previous years. In fact, FORI seems so easy that you may be tempted to treat it casually, but recent research has shown that without sufficient attention to text length, time-on-task, and purposeful implementation of the procedures, the approach quickly loses its effectiveness. Conversely, when teachers implement the approach with adequate attention to details, the program is more effective than alternatives such as round-robin reading or reader's workshop.

Allowing for some variability in terms of the number of days it takes to cover a given selection (i.e., longer texts may require additional days), we have found that the five-day lesson plan presented in Table 3.1 and explained in the lesson snapshot works well with most texts, no matter what the source (i.e., literature anthologies, basal readers, or trade books). Further, teachers have found the FORI format to be very helpful in a number of ways: first, it provides students access to material that would be too difficult for them to read on their own, thereby exposing them to richer vocabulary and a broader range of concepts than they would otherwise have access to; second, the students tend to enjoy the regularity of the procedure (for example, on several occasions, we have seen

Table 3.1

Fluency-Oriented Reading Instruction

Monday (Day 1)	Tuesday (Day 2)	Wednesday (Day 3)	Thursday (Day 4)	Friday (Day 5)
• Teacher introduces selection to class using prereading activities • Teacher reads the selection to class while class follows along • Teacher and class discuss selection to develop text comprehension	• Teacher and students echo read selection • Comprehension should be developed through various strategies such as teacher and student questioning, visualization, etc.	• Teacher and students choral read selection • Additional comprehension activities can be undertaken, but the primary focus of Day 3 is the choral reading of the text	• Students partner read selection • Additional comprehension activities can be undertaken, but the primary focus of Day 4 is the partner reading of the text	• Students complete postreading extension activities • Activities may include writing in response to story, discussion of character motivations, summarization, etc.

kids come in and ask, "today is partner [or choral or echo] reading, isn't it?"); and third, teachers find that the structure reduces the stress of trying to create entirely new lesson plans on a weekly basis.

Lesson Snapshot

The FORI procedure usually follows a five-day lesson plan, allowing you to cover approximately one story per week, as follows:

Day 1

■ Introduce each week's selection with the prereading activities that you would normally use to introduce a story. These can include teaching key vocabulary words, making predictions, or developing the students' background knowledge regarding the subject matter.

- Read the text aloud while students follow along in their own copy. It is important to circulate around the room to ensure that your students are following along. Further, some students may need to track the print as you read to them. This helps them follow along with your reading and keeps them from getting lost or becoming stuck on an unfamiliar word or phrase.

- Engage your students in a discussion of the story by extending the text (what do you think happened to the characters after the story ended?); discussing character motivation (why do you think a given character made a particular choice?); or developing your students' empathy (would you have made the same decision as the character in a given situation? why or why not?). This first day focuses your students' attention on two important elements of literacy learning: the fluent rendering of a text and the construction of meaning.

- Students should read a book of their own choosing for homework.

Day 2

- Conduct an echo reading of the text with your students (see Chapter 1 for an explanation of the echo reading procedure). If your learners are already familiar with the process of echo reading, try longer chunks of text, at least a paragraph or two at a time, so that they are not relying on their verbal memory to echo the text back to you. If this is their first encounter with echo reading, make sure to only read a sentence or two before asking them to echo the text, at least until they become comfortable with the procedure. This should take only a few weeks. As the students become familiar with the process, start to expand the amount of material being read to a paragraph or two—or as much as a page, if either your students are very comfortable with the process or the layout of the selection is such that the amount of text on a single page is not overwhelming. And remember to circulate around the

continued

room to guarantee that students are participating in the reading of the text and not reciting from memory.

- Another vital piece of the second day's instruction involves ensuring that your readers focus on the meaning of the selection and not just on word recognition. This can be accomplished in several ways. For instance, you can integrate questions within the text at appropriate pausing points to check that students understand the meaning of a new vocabulary word or a particular event. Alternatively, ask students to summarize sections of texts in pairs, with each partner taking a turn in revolving order. Or have students create questions to ask each other about the story and give them the opportunity to pose their questions to their peers. A number of comprehension strategies could work at this point in the lesson; for example, see Cooper and Kiger (2005) or Gunning (2002).

- Students should also take the text home and read the story aloud to a family member or friend for additional practice starting on Day 2.

Day 3

- The third day is the shortest in terms of the amount of time spent reading the text. On this day, choral read the selections with your students. Choral reading simply involves you and your students' reading the text in unison (see Chapter 1 for a description of the choral reading procedure); however, pay particular attention to students who may experience trouble keeping up with their peers. As was suggested for the preceding days, it is helpful to circulate around the room, refocusing students who have lost their place simply by pointing out where the class is reading or by making sure they are looking at the material rather than out the window!

- At this point, what students read for homework depends on how fluently they appear to be reading the week's primary selection. If they seem to be fairly comfortable with the text, you can give them the option of reading something of their own choosing. If, on the other hand, they seem to need additional practice, ask them to reread the main selection out loud to a family member or friend.

Day 4

■ The final reading of the story incorporates a partner reading of the selection. Partner reading involves dividing the class into pairs of readers and having each member of the pair read alternate pages of text (see Chapter 1 for a description of effective partner reading procedures as well as ways to select partners). Because the students have already covered the material at least three times, if one reader experiences difficulty with the text, their partner will likely be able to provide assistance. You should once again circulate among the students during this period in order to provide additional help as needed. Once partners have completed reading the text, and if time allows, they can reread the material again; however, on this second reading students should read the pages opposite those they read earlier to ensure that both children read the entire text at least once during this period.

■ For homework, follow the outline for Day 3: students who are reading the primary text fluently can read a text of their own choosing, whereas struggling readers read the week's selection one last time.

Day 5

■ The final day of the weekly lesson plan consists of extension activities to develop a richer understanding of the text; these can include student-led discussions (perhaps following a literature circle model), written responses or alternative endings to the text, or an artistic response to the selection (see Cooper and Kiger [2005] or Gunning [2002], for examples of additional comprehension activities).

■ Students can read a book of their own choosing for homework.

Wide Fluency-Oriented Reading Instruction (Wide FORI)

The other whole-class approach is that of Wide Fluency-Oriented Reading Instruction (Wide FORI; Kuhn et al., 2006). As mentioned earlier, when Steven Stahl and I (2003) reviewed the research on fluency instruction, it appeared to us that the scaffolded reading of many texts frequently produced outcomes similar to the repeated reading of a single text. Further studies conducted with second graders have indicated that Wide Reading[1] is highly effective at improving reading fluency. As with the FORI approach, Wide FORI is heavily scaffolded. Unlike the FORI approach, which involves the repeated reading of a single text, Wide FORI involves reading multiple texts over the course of a week.

Because Wide FORI calls for three sets of texts over the course of each week, you may need to be creative to ensure you have enough reading material available for your learners. For the original study (Kuhn et al., 2006), each class used the school's basal reader or literature anthology as the week's first selection and grade-level trade books for the second and third texts. Based on this format, if your class is currently using a basal program or a literature anthology, its selections can serve as your primary text each week. It is likely to be more difficult to procure two class sets of trade books for each week of the school year, so you may need to do some creative thinking to find enough selections to undertake this program. For example, if your school is using a guided reading program, it is likely that, between your colleagues and the school library, you will be able to find enough copies of a given book to create a class set. One school we worked with was able to locate twenty-four copies of *Frog and Toad Are Friends* (Lobel, 1970) this way. Older versions of basals may also be stored somewhere in the school, perhaps in a storage closet or in the basement, and these

could be used as an additional text. Further, schools often sub-
scribe to student magazines such as *My Weekly Reader* or *National
Geographic Kids*; these contain substantive articles, both in terms of
content and length, that can be used for a reading. Finally, grade-
appropriate material can be downloaded from the Internet, and
copies can be made for each student in the class.

Despite the differences between the number of texts used, the
FORI and Wide FORI approaches have several similarities: Wide
FORI is also a five-day program that is relatively easy to implement as part of your shared reading program; comprehension is
brought to the fore in both methods; both programs call for students to spend at least twenty to thirty minutes per day reading
connected text; and classroom-based research has also shown the
Wide FORI approach to be successful (Kuhn et al., 2006). In a recent
study, students using the Wide FORI and FORI approaches made
significantly greater growth on standardized measures of comprehension and word recognition in isolation than did their peers who
used alternative reading methods. Interestingly, the students in
the Wide FORI group also did better than their peers in either the
FORI or the other reading groups in terms of correct words read
per minute. This indicates that, while both the FORI and the Wide
FORI approaches are effective, the use of multiple texts may be
preferable. As a result, we recommend the Wide FORI approach as
our first choice, if it is at all possible for you to implement it within
your classroom.

Teachers have generally found that the lesson plans provided
for this approach are an effective way to incorporate three selections into a typical school week. Note, however, that if you are
using lengthy selections, you may not be able to cover three texts
within the five-day lesson plan described in the lesson snapshot and
outlined in Table 3.2. Since the use of multiple texts offers learners
access to a broader range of vocabulary and concepts than does a

Table 3.2

Wide Reading

Monday (Day 1)	Tuesday (Day 2)	Wednesday (Day 3)	Thursday (Day 4)	Friday (Day 5)
• Teacher introduces selection to class using prereading activities • Teacher reads the selection to class while class follows along • Teacher and class discuss selection to develop text comprehension	• Teacher and students echo read the first selection • Comprehension should be developed through various strategies such as teacher and student questioning, visualization, etc. • If time allows, a second reading (choral or partner) should take place	• Students complete postreading extension activities • Activities may include writing in response to story, discussion of character motivations, summarization, etc.	• Teacher and students echo read a second selection • Comprehension should be developed through various strategies such as teacher and student questioning, predicting, etc. • If time allows a choral or partner reading of the second selection can occur • Students can complete postreading extension activities	• Teacher and students echo read a third selection • Comprehension should be developed through various strategies such as teacher and student questioning, predicting, etc. • If time allows a choral or partner reading of the third selection can occur • Students can complete postreading extension activities

single selection, the Wide FORI approach may better counter the gap that begins to occur as early as the primary grades between more skilled readers and their struggling peers. By helping all students become skilled readers, this procedure aids in laying the groundwork for independent reading success in later grades. As with all the fluency approaches presented in this book, it is critical that these texts be substantial enough to deserve the focus of a twenty- to forty-minute daily reading lesson.

Lesson Snapshot

The five-day procedure focuses on one primary text—and incorporates a limited amount of repetition for that selection, after which a single reading of the second and third texts is typical:

Day 1

- Day 1 parallels that of the FORI approach. Begin by introducing each week's selection with the prereading activities that you would normally use. These can include building background knowledge, making predictions, and preteaching important vocabulary words that the students will encounter as they read the text.

- Next, you should read the text aloud while your students follow along in their own copy. Since some students may drift off-task during your reading, it is important to circulate around the room to ensure students are following along. It may also be necessary to have some students track what is being read as you read to them.

- End the first day's lesson with an engaged discussion of the selection among you and your students. As with the FORI approach, the goals for Day 1 are to provide your students with a fluent rendering of the text and to develop their comprehension of the material (see Day 1 of the FORI approach for some ideas for the discussion).

- Students should read a book of their own choosing for homework.

Day 2

- On Day 2, conduct an echo reading of the text with your students. As explained earlier, if your learners are familiar with

continued

this process, begin by reading passages between a paragraph or two and a page long so that your students are not relying on their verbal memory. But if your students are unfamiliar with this procedure, start by reading only a sentence or two and build up to longer passages over the course of several weeks.

■ In addition to giving your students the opportunity to develop their word recognition, it is also important that you work on expanding your readers' comprehension of the selection on Day 2. As was discussed for the FORI component, a number of comprehension strategies could work here, including embedding teacher-directed questions within the text, summarization, and the use of student-created questions at predetermined stopping points (see Cooper and Kiger [2005] or Gunning [2002] for further suggestions).

■ Finally, if there is time, the students can partner read the text at this point as well.

■ On Day 2, the homework should consist of reading the text aloud to a family member or friend for additional practice.

Day 3

■ The Wide FORI approach begins to diverge from its FORI counterpart on Day 3. Rather than rereading the primary text again, the focus is on postreading. A number of extension activities can be employed to further develop your students' comprehension at this point (see Cooper and Kiger [2005] or Gunning [2002] for further suggestions).

■ What students read for homework on Day 3 depends on their fluency with the week's primary text. If they appear to be fairly fluent with the selection, they should choose another text they want to read, however, if they appear to need additional practice, ask them to reread the primary text again.

Days 4 and 5

- The fourth and fifth days parallel one another and involve the echo reading of the second and third texts. Since you may only read these texts once as a class, it is important that you focus on comprehension of the stories as well, either through a structured activity, such as the Directed Reading Thinking Activity, or through informal questioning and discussion.

- If there is sufficient time on a given day, have the students read the texts a second time, either by choral or partner reading the selection.

- Students should also read each of these texts aloud to a family member or friend for homework on Thursday (the second text) and Friday (the third text) in order to receive additional practice.

Conducting Effective Whole-Class Instruction—Some Final Thoughts

Before leaving these two approaches, we would like to emphasize some final thoughts. These approaches have helped promote the fluency development of second graders across several studies (Kuhn et al., 2006; Stahl & Heubach, 2005; Schwanenflugel et al., under review) and have set the stage for fluency development in several ways. Both make use of challenging material that exposes children to a variety of concepts, vocabulary, and ideas that might not be accessible through instructional-level texts. Exposure to such texts also helps to establish ideas and phrases in students' memory and leads to better fluency and comprehension of future texts (Logan, 1997). Further, these programs provide students with extensive scaffolding as they read these texts; and both programs require children to spend at least twenty to forty minutes per day focusing on complex texts.

Finally, both programs include at least some repeated reading, a procedure that has also been shown to improve text comprehension (Walczyk et al., 2004). However, of the two methods, the Wide FORI approach has been more consistent in accelerating learners' fluency and comprehension, so we recommend it as the preferred approach if at all possible.

Study Guide Questions

- How does the use of repetition help students become fluent readers?

- How does the reading of multiple texts with support also assist students in becoming fluent readers?

- Do you think repetition or wide reading might benefit comprehension more? Why?

- Of the two approaches to shared reading presented in this chapter, which do you think would work best in your classroom? Why?

- Select one of your shared reading texts and think through how it could be used as part of a FORI or Wide Reading lesson. Is it sufficiently complex and lengthy for the approach? What prereading activities would you use to facilitate understanding? What questions could you ask to begin discussion? What questions could you embed in the echo reading to deepen your students' comprehension? What extension activities would be appropriate for the selection?

Notes

1. Wide Reading incorporates any single scaffolded reading of texts that allow students to spend substantial amounts of time reading with support and differs from a more general use of wide reading where students simple read large amounts of texts on their own.

Chapter 4

Fluency and Differentiated Instruction
Working with Flexible Groups

Instructional Approach	Grade Levels	Grouping	Type of Text
Oral Recitation Lesson	• Originally grade 2 • Can be used with grade 3 and above	• Originally small-group instruction • Can be used for whole-class instruction depending on the selections and students' needs	Longer, challenging texts, including basals, chapter books, novels, speeches, longer poems, etc. (20–30 minutes reading per day)
Fluency-Oriented Oral Reading	• Originally grade 2 • Can be used with grade 3 and above	• Originally small-group instruction • Can be used as a supplement for whole-class instruction • Can be used in a tutorial situation with one or two students	Challenging texts including short chapter books, longer poems, speeches, etc. (15–20 minutes reading per lesson)
Wide Fluency-Oriented Oral Reading	• Originally grade 2 • Can be used with grade 3 and above	• Originally small-group instruction • Can be used as a supplement for whole-class instruction • Can be used in a tutorial situation with one or two students	Challenging texts including short chapter books, longer poems, speeches, etc. (15–20 minutes reading per lesson)
Supported Oral Reading	• Originally grade 2 • Primary and elementary grades (excluding first)	• Originally small-group instruction • Can be used as a supplement for whole-class instruction	Longer, challenging texts, including basals, chapter books, novels, speeches, longer poems, etc. (20–30 minutes reading per day)

- What role does fluency play in differentiated instruction?

- What approaches to fluency instruction are effective for flexible grouping?

Fluency Instruction for Flexible Groups

Given that most students make the transition to fluent reading around the second and third grades (e.g., Chall, 1996), it makes sense that strategies designed for your whole class are most appropriate for those learners. However, you will find that some students in the early grades are already fairly fluent readers and others are still working on basics such as concepts of print and phonemic awareness. As such, fluency approaches such as Wide Reading and FORI are not going to be the best option for these students. Similarly, you may have groups of older readers who have not made the transition to fluent reading and who would benefit from instruction that focuses on this area, even though these strategies would not be appropriate for your whole class. In terms of text level as well, you may find that what constitutes challenging text for some of your learners is not sufficiently challenging for others or, on the opposite end of the spectrum, some material may actually be so challenging for a group of your students that they will not be able to benefit from its use no matter how much scaffolding you incorporate. In any of these situations, you will likely want to use **flexible grouping** as a means of meeting the varied needs of your learners.

One option is to use the Wide FORI or FORI (Kuhn et al., 2006) approaches discussed in the previous chapter with smaller groups. The weekly lesson plans for both methods are readily adaptable.

One teacher divided her class into two groups to ensure that her most struggling readers had greater opportunities for support. By dividing the class into a small group of struggling readers (about six students) and a larger group of students (about eighteen) who were not experiencing such difficulties, she was able to better meet the needs of all her students. Several other approaches can also help you meet your needs within a flexible grouping format. These methods are designed specifically for small groups of learners and can assume a more adaptable role in your overall literacy curriculum as a result. The principles of support, modeling, focus on phrasing, extensive opportunity for practice (Rasinski, 2003), and use of challenging text (e.g., Kuhn, 2005) nevertheless remain critical components of these practices—whether you are working with students in the second and third grade or readers in grade four and beyond.

Oral Recitation Lesson (ORL)

The Oral Recitation Lesson (ORL) is a seminal method designed by Jim Hoffman (1987), along with Susan Crone (Hoffman & Crone, 1985), that has served as a model for many of the approaches in both this chapter and the proceeding one (so the framework may seem familiar). The authors were searching for alternative approaches to round-robin reading in order to make more effective use of basal readers. After exploring oral reading practices from the nineteenth century, they found two forms of literacy instruction that seemed particularly relevant: the recitation lesson and the story method. Both approaches were effective at developing expressive reading and increasing comprehension among readers, so Hoffman and Crone designed the Oral Recitation Lesson around the principles found in these two methods. The ORL was initially developed for groups of second graders who were experiencing difficulties reading their grade-level basals; however, by using speeches or literature as your reading material, ORL can readily be adapted for a broader range of students, including students beyond the second and third grade.

According to the authors, three principles were central to the effectiveness of the recitation lesson and the story method. First is comprehension, which was dealt with early in the lessons to emphasize its role as the primary reason for reading; this is particularly important for struggling readers, who often develop the mistaken notion that the main goal of reading is word identification. By focusing students on comprehension early in the lesson, you increase the likelihood they will learn that accurate word recognition is important only insofar as it allows access to a text's meaning. Second is modeling. Before asking the students to read the text themselves, teachers were expected to model the material by reading it aloud as the students followed along. This was important because it provided the learners with a prosodic interpretation of the material and allowed them to hear the text being read accurately and automatically. Third is repetition, which was used to scaffold the learners' reading as they developed comfort with the text.

When reflecting on the ORL's initial implementation, Jim Hoffman noted, "many of the basal reader stories could be described as non-stories" (1987, p. 371) with minimal plot and character development and limited vocabulary and language structures. While this remains a problem with some materials currently in use, recent editions of literature anthologies and basal readers by and large incorporate more sophisticated text selections, minimizing the likelihood of encountering this particular problem. If you do find that selections in your reading program are not substantive enough to merit a significant proportion of your class time, I suggest that you find alternative sources of material to serve as the basis of this ORL instruction. These can range from science or social studies textbooks to trade books to weekly student magazines that make use of more natural language and more complex concepts.

Lesson Snapshot

The Oral Recitation Lesson was intended to create effective instruction using narrative selections from the basal readers that were the dominant instructional materials of the 1980s, but it can be used with any material that is of reasonable length and is appropriately challenging for your readers. The procedure itself incorporates five components divided into two basic phases, which should occur over several days, or possibly a school week, depending on the length and complexity of the selection. The first phase, direct instruction, incorporates a comprehension, a practice, and a performance component. The second phase, indirect instruction, involves practicing to mastery.

- The procedure begins with the comprehension component, in which you read a selection aloud to your class. Use appropriate expression and phrasing so your students can hear the pronunciation of any unknown words and where appropriate breaks occur. This models the type of oral reading you will be expecting from them. By providing them with the opportunity to hear the text as a whole, you are also building their understanding of the selection in its entirety. Since the students will eventually be responsible for reading a section of the text themselves, it is critical that they follow along in their own copy of the selection. By circulating around the room, you can note whether your students are following along and redirect any of them who have lost their place or are off-task. It may also be helpful for you to introduce your students to the text prior to your initial reading by using prereading activities, such as asking prediction questions, building background knowledge, and introducing unknown vocabulary words.

- Following completion of the reading, you and your students should discuss the story in order to expand their understanding of the material. In the original intervention designed by

continued

Hoffman and Crone, this involved constructing a story map with the students (e.g., identifying the setting, characters, main events, and resolution), but a number of other comprehension-based activities would also be appropriate choices. For example, you and your students could create a summary of the selection, discuss character motivation, or generate drawings based on the key events or important points in the readings.

- The second component of the direct instruction phase involves various fluency strategies. Depending on how much assistance your students need, you could ask them to echo or choral read the selection (it is worth noting that echo reading provides more scaffolding than does choral reading; see Chapter 1 for a detailed description of these two strategies). This component is meant to reemphasize prosodic reading and move students away from the word-by-word reading common to disfluent readers and toward reading that incorporates appropriate expression, phrasing, and automatic word recognition. Should you feel that your students would benefit from additional supported readings, you can revisit this step before moving on to the next component, performance.

- In the final component of the direct instruction phase, students select and practice a section of the text; in Hoffman and Crone's original study, the length of these sections was usually about one page, but this may vary depending on the amount of text per page and the reading ability of your learners. This independent practice not only allows the students to develop their fluency, but also gives them the opportunity to create their own interpretation of the text. Once students become comfortable reading their selection, they can choose to read it aloud to their classmates. Peers are invited to provide positive feedback for the reader. However, if a student does not want to read aloud in front of other children, don't force him. As students see their friends perform, they will likely develop a willingness to read aloud themselves.

- The second phase of the ORL, indirect instruction, involves additional practice on the stories being used by the class. This component was added to Hoffman and Crone's original intervention because the students, all of whom were struggling readers, required the extra practice in order to master the passage. During this phase, students who have not achieved mastery of their passage are asked to practice the selection they are working on for ten minutes a day. They are expected to practice the text until they are able to read it with at least 98 percent accuracy, at a rate of seventy-five correct words per minute or higher, and with appropriate expression. If some of your learners could benefit from additional practice, you may want to integrate this component into your curriculum during your classroom "down times," perhaps in the mornings before lessons get under way or during independent reading period. Your students should reread their section of the text using either mumble or **whisper reading** and should be encouraged to take copies of the stories home for extra practice as well. Once they have achieved the established criteria with a given text, urge them to begin reading a book of their own choosing until the class begins to work with their next selection.

- This extra practice was deemed unnecessary for students who were not struggling. Should you use a more challenging text with these readers, the indirect instruction component may be a necessary addition to your lessons for all your students.

Fluency-Oriented Oral Reading (FOOR) and Wide Fluency-Oriented Oral Reading (Wide FOOR)

The next approaches, Fluency-Oriented Oral Reading (FOOR) and Wide Fluency-Oriented Oral Reading (Wide FOOR) (Kuhn, 2005), were designed to explore repetition versus **scaffolded wide reading,** or reading a variety of texts with significant support (see Chapter 3 for a discussion of the role both types of instruction play in fluency development). As with many other fluency methods, I designed the intervention to use challenging text that required significant amounts of scaffolding. Since I was working with struggling second grade readers, this meant using texts ranging from a late-first- to an early-third-grade reading level (e.g., Gunning, 1997; Fountas & Pinnell, 1999), and included titles such as *The Fire Cat* (Averill, 1988), *The Case of the Dumb Bells* (Bonsall, 1982), and *Whistle for Willie* (Keats, 1977) (for a list of all the titles used in the original study, see Table 4.1). But this approach is readily adapted for work with small groups of older readers. Just remember to select reading material that is appropriately challenging for your students' reading level.

In order to determine the effectiveness of FOOR and Wide FOOR for small-group instruction, I initially worked with four groups of five or six second graders, although you could have fewer students in the group, and it would certainly be possible to use these procedures in a one-on-one tutoring situation. I met three times a week for approximately fifteen to twenty minutes per session with three of the groups. The first group used a modified repeated readings technique, or Fluency-Oriented Oral Reading (FOOR). This consisted of my echo or choral reading a single trade book three times over the course of a week with the students (i.e., we read the same book each time we met). With the second group, I used Wide Fluency-Oriented Oral Reading (Wide FOOR); this involved echo or choral reading three different texts per week, or one new text for each session. The third group simply listened to the same stories used with the Wide FOOR students, but were not provided with their own copy of the texts. The fourth group did not receive any extra reading instruction beyond what was occurring during their classroom literacy instruction.

While the approaches were fairly straightforward, the results were quite interesting. To begin with, both the FOOR and the Wide

Table 4.1

Books Used for Intervention

The Golly Sisters Go West (1985) by Betsy Byars (K)*
Hooray for the Golly Sisters! (1990) by Betsy Byars (K)
Whistle for Willie (1977) by Jack Ezra Keats (L)*
Harry the Dirty Dog (1984) by Gene Zion (2)
Big Max (1992) by Kin Platt (J)*
The Fire Cat (1988) by Esther Averill (J)
Amelia Bedelia (1992) by Peggy Parish (L)
Come Back, Amelia Bedelia (1995) by Peggy Parish (K)*
Frog and Toad Are Friends (1970) by Arnold Lobel (K)
Frog and Toad Together (1979) by Arnold Lobel (K)*
Bedtime for Frances (1995) by Russell Hoban (K)
The Case of the Dumb Bells (1982) by Crosby Bonsall (K)*
The Case of the Cat's Meow (1978) by Crosby Bonsall (K)
Arthur's Funny Money (1984) by Lillian Hoban (K)
Arthur's Prize Reader (1984) by Lillian Hoban (K)
Aunt Eater Loves a Mystery (1987) by Doug Cushman (K)
Aunt Eater's Mystery Vacation (1993) by Doug Cushman (K)
The Case of the Two Masked Robbers (1988) by Lillian Hoban (K)

Note: Titles marked with an asterisk indicate books read by Fluency-Oriented Oral Reading group; the remaining texts were used by the Wide Reading Instruction group and the Listening-Only group. Letters represent guided reading levels (Fountas & Pinnell, 1999).

FOOR groups did better than either the students who simply listened to the texts or the students who did not get any additional literacy instruction on measures that looked at word recognition in isolation, prosody, and correct words per minute. Further, the Wide FOOR group made greater growth in terms of comprehension than any of the other groups. It seems possible that this last result may be due to the types of tasks required by the differing reading approaches; while there was some discussion of the readings during these sessions, there was no specific comprehension instruction. Consequently, the students may have developed their own sense of what to focus on during the lessons. That is, since repetition was used in the FOOR group, the students in that group may have thought they were rereading a single text per week primarily to improve their word recognition and prosody, whereas the students in the Wide FOOR group may have thought they were reading multiple texts to construct meaning as well. It may be that such differences in implicit purposes are reflected in the differing outcomes on the measure of comprehension. It is important to note that similar results have been found in other repeated reading studies (e.g., O'Shea, Sindelar, & O'Shea, 1985, 1987) and that merely by asking students to focus on the meaning of the story, student comprehension has improved. Given this, it may be that by adding a meaning-focus to the lessons, the students in the FOOR group could have made gains in comprehension similar to those made by the students in the Wide FOOR group.

Both FOOR and Wide FOOR can be used as part of a flexible grouping format with anywhere from two to six students or in a one-on-one tutorial setting across grade levels, starting in second grade. The approaches are based on a Monday-Wednesday-Friday schedule, although any days are fine so long as students are given the opportunity to read challenging material with support for significant periods of time (fifteen to twenty minutes per session).

You can use these approaches throughout the school year, but you should reevaluate how well the students are able to read material at a given level every few weeks. This will allow you to determine when the students are ready to advance to the next reading level; it is essential that you keep raising the reading level of the texts so that the material remains challenging. These evaluations will also tell you when students are ready for grade-level material as their instructional level text. At this point, you will need to determine whether to maintain a fluency component as part of their reading instruction or whether an alternative focus, say on comprehension instruction, may be more beneficial. The answer to this may, in fact, be complicated. Even if your learners are fairly fluent with grade-level material, you may want to continue with this instructional strand in order to further solidify their reading fluency. On the other hand, if students have become comfortable with grade-level material, it may be more productive to minimize or even eliminate their fluency instruction. What you decide will depend on the varying needs of each group of learners and is likely to change from year to year.

Lesson Snapshot

Day 1 (FOOR and Wide FOOR)

- Briefly discuss what the story may be about based on the title and the cover of the book. Since you are likely to have a limited amount of time, and since the focus of this activity is to develop reading fluency, comprehension should be dealt with as you read the text rather than through distinct instructional activities.

- Echo read the selection with your students. As your students' word recognition improves, switch occasionally to choral

continued

reading for the initial reading (see Chapter 1 for a more in-depth discussion of these strategies).

- Interweave questions as you go through the story, stopping occasionally to ask students to predict or clarify the story, and explain new or interesting words or terms as you encounter them. After completing the story, you can involve your students in a short, informal discussion of the story.

- If time allows, complete either a second echo or choral reading of the story or a section of the story.

Days 2 and 3 (Wide FOOR)

- The second and third days of the Wide FOOR approach follow the same procedure as on Day 1, but with a second and third text. This material could include sets of books taken from a guided reading program, selections from a basal series or literature anthology, trade books garnered from the school and classroom libraries, student magazines, or selections gathered from websites. As long as the material remains challenging and all the students have their own copies, virtually any type of text can be used.

Day 2 (FOOR)

- On the second day of the FOOR procedure, have the students partner read the week's selection (see Chapter 1 for a more detailed discussion of this procedure). Students should work in pairs with one student reading the even pages and the other student reading the odd pages. Because there will be a maximum of three pairs of students, you can easily circulate and assist students with any difficulty they encounter. Alternatively, you can act as a partner for one of the students should there be any absences. After the students have completed the first partner reading of the story, if there is enough time, they can switch pages and read through all or part of the text for a second time.

Day 3 (FOOR)

- On the third day, lead the students in a final choral reading of the story (again, see Chapter 1 for a further explanation of this approach). By this point, they should be fairly familiar with the text. If you feel students need greater support, echo read the selection with them instead. After completing this last rereading of the text, ask the students to volunteer to read a section of the material or complete a running record with each of your learners to determine how their reading of the text has developed.

Supported Oral Reading

Darrel Morris and Laurie Nelson (1992) have also created a successful fluency intervention for group instruction. Supported Oral Reading was originally designed for second graders whose reading was significantly below average, but has the potential to be used with other age groups. The authors developed the approach for an inner-city classroom where half of the class was reading below the primer level. The size of the discrepancy between the students' instructional level and their grade level led the authors to design a strategy that not only incorporated significant amounts of scaffolding but could also be implemented as part of the general literacy curriculum. The Supported Oral Reading lesson initially consisted of two twenty-minute sessions per week. During the first session the teacher and the students echo read a story; this was followed with the students' independent rereading of the selection at the second session.

However, the authors soon realized that one session of scaffolded reading did not adequately prepare students for the task of reading the text on their own. As a result, they rethought the design of their intervention and decided to increase the number of weekly sessions to three, to incorporate the elements of modeling and discussion, and to increase the opportunities for student practice. These modifications helped ensure that the students had the support and practice necessary to read their assigned texts independently. According to Morris and Nelson, improvements in the students' reading could be seen in terms of rate, accuracy, and overall reading levels—not only for the passages practiced in class but for nonpracticed material as well. Moreover, all the participating students made gains on measures of word recognition, eight of the ten made significant gains on the Diagnostic Reading Scales, and their scores on the Iowa Test of Basic Skills (ITBS) ranged from 1.5 to 2.2—quite solid growth, given that these students were reading below the primer level at the beginning of the school year.

The three-day procedure can be integrated into your flexible grouping component most easily on an every-other-day schedule (e.g., Monday, Wednesday, and Friday). As the authors determined in their work with struggling readers, the lessons must be implemented at least three days a week if students are to develop sufficient comfort with one text before moving on to another. As with other approaches discussed in this book, challenging material should be used. It is important that each student have his or her own copy of the text, but since you are not working with your entire class, consider sources of material beyond the shared reading texts you use for whole-class instruction. By identifying a variety of resources, you are guaranteeing that your students work with at least two different selections per week: the text you use for their primary literacy instruction and a second text for their Supported Oral Reading lessons. Research on wide reading shows that using multiple texts provides students with access to a broader range of vocabulary and concepts than is the case with a single text.

If you find that the students are not making adequate progress following this lesson plan, try adding an additional session prior to Day 2 (partner reading), in which you echo or choral read the text with the students again in order to give them extra practice. Remember as the students' reading develops over the course of the year to provide them with increasingly challenging texts. Otherwise, the material will begin to represent their independent reading level and any further gains will be minimal. It is worth noting that the students in the original study demonstrated a positive attitude toward the sessions and that their attitude toward reading in general improved as well. Ultimately, that is the best possible outcome for any approach to reading instruction.

Lesson Snapshot

Day 1

- Begin the Supported Oral Reading lesson by expressively reading the week's selection to your students while they follow along in their own copies.

- As with most of the other approaches presented thus far, follow up with a discussion to develop your students' comprehension of the material—a process that allows the text to be dealt with as a whole.

- After completing the discussion, you and your students should either echo or mumble read the text (see Chapter 1 for a more in-depth discussion of echo reading). This ensures that your students have had the opportunity to read the text in a supported manner prior to attempting to read it independently.

Day 2

- The second day incorporates one, and possibly two, partner readings of the selection (see Chapter 1 for a more detailed

continued

discussion of this procedure). The children work in pairs for this activity, reading alternate pages of text.

■ After completing the first partner reading of the text, ask students to select and practice a hundred-word passage from the story. They can practice their passage by mumble or whisper reading the selection quietly or by reading into "phones" that direct the students' voices back to themselves (these can either be made with PVC pipes or bought at many educational supply stores).

■ At the end of the session, if time permits, the students can re-form into pairs for a second partner reading of the text—this time with each partner focusing on the pages opposite those they read initially.

Day 3

■ On the final day, provide your students with an opportunity to read aloud the passage they practiced while you take a **running record** of their rendition. If the students still appear to be disfluent, you can ask them to continue to practice the selection over the weekend. If their reading is smooth and expressive, encourage them to read a book or some other text of their own choosing for homework.

Conducting Effective Instruction with Flexible Groups—Some Final Thoughts

Because the pace of your students' literacy development is likely to fluctuate, especially as students move into the upper elementary grades and beyond, integrating fluency instruction into flexible reading groups may be the best way to meet the needs of all your learners. This will allow you to vary your curriculum so that oral reading instruction is targeted to those who will most benefit from it. If you choose to use the approaches outlined in this chapter, remember that oral reading instruction should not be the entirety of your students' literacy curriculum, but instead serve as one element within it. Further, as students become increasingly fluent with text at a given reading level, it is important to use increasingly challenging material. As your learners become comfortable with text that is at or even somewhat above their grade level, you can phase out fluency-oriented instruction and replace it with additional comprehension instruction, writing activities, or even the opportunity to read an expanded range of fiction and informational texts.

Study Guide Questions

- Do you think fluency instruction is appropriate for some of your students but not others? If so, which ones? Or do you think that most of your students would benefit from some form of fluency instruction? What constitutes challenging texts variation by group?

- Which of the strategies listed in this chapter do you think would be most effective for your learners? Would you use the same approach for all the groups or would you use different strategies for different groups?

- Think about your class; how would you group your students for fluency instruction? Think about your groups; which approaches would you use with each of these different groups? Which texts would you use with the different groups (remembering that the texts used for fluency instruction need to be sufficiently challenging to warrant the amount of scaffolding provided by these approaches)?

- Select one of the approaches that you would like to use with one (or several) of your groups, along with an appropriate text. How would you go about implementing the method you selected with this particular group of students?

Chapter 5

Fluency Instruction for Pairs and Individual Learners

Instructional Approach	Grade Levels	Grouping	Type of Text
Repeated Reading	Struggling readers at any grade level (excluding first)	One-on-one tutoring	Challenging texts
Neurological Impress Method (NIM)	Struggling readers at any grade level (excluding first)	One-on-one tutoring	Challenging texts
Reading-While-Listening	Struggling readers at any grade level (excluding first)	Center activity	Challenging texts
Cross-Age Reading	Struggling readers at any grade level (excluding first)	Center activity (resulting in a rendering of the text for younger students or a recording of the material for a center)	Texts at the students' instructional levels

- What is the role of fluency instruction in tutoring?

- What approaches for fluency instruction are designed for individual learners and pairs of students?

- Which strategies can be integrated into literacy centers?

What If Only One or Two Students Need Fluency Instruction?

Many times when you are working with older students (fourth grade and above), only one or two need fluency-oriented instruction. Or you may be working as a reading specialist, in which case you have the opportunity to work with students in pairs or in a one-on-one tutoring situation. Alternatively, you may be a classroom teacher who is tutoring a few of her second and third graders after school, during lunch, or before classes begin in the morning. If you find yourself working in any of these environments, gearing instruction to the specific needs of your learners is easier than it would be in a classroom because you have the advantage of identifying texts that are just right for each situation. You can provide your learners with specific texts for reading they are to do on their own (independent level texts), for comprehension and decoding activities (instructional level texts), and for their fluency-oriented reading (challenging texts).

While it is quite likely that you will spend at least part of your time in a tutorial situation developing your learners' word recognition strategies and comprehension, you will probably use some of the time working on their fluency development as well. Fortunately, a number of fluency-oriented instructional approaches are designed specifically for pairs of readers (dyads) or individual learners. While most of these strategies involve repetition, prior to discussing them, I would like to stress the value of simply reading with a student or a pair of students for at least a portion of your instructional time. It is often the case that older disfluent readers do not have sufficient opportunities to read texts at any level. This is true for texts at their independent level, because they feel embarrassed reading books that are written for "babies," and it is true for most material assigned as part of their coursework, since such texts are usually too challenging for these students to attempt on their own. In fact, teachers who work with large groups of older struggling readers generally forego assigning texts altogether, turning instead to lectures as the only viable means of expanding their learners' knowledge base; whereas teachers who have only a few disfluent readers in the classroom find that, due to a lack of time or access to appropriate methods, these kids can "fall through the cracks."

If you are lucky enough to work with students either individually or in pairs, one of the best ways to provide them with access to texts while simultaneously building their fluency is simply to read aloud together. Take turns reading aloud a paragraph or a page of text at a time or choral or echo read selections to prevent monotony (see Chapter 1 for explanations of these approaches). Whichever format you choose, I have found that most students really enjoy this opportunity, especially if they have input regarding the choice of text (although students can also benefit from being introduced to selections they may not consider on their own). You may be concerned that this recommendation stands in stark contrast to my earlier warnings about reading unpracticed text aloud; however, it is important to note there are three differences between these processes and round-robin reading. First, when you are reading with one or two other readers, each of you would be reading approximately one-third to one-half of the text; so, rather than one minute of reading, give or take, for every thirty minutes of class time, each participant (you and one or two students) would be reading connected text for approximately ten to fifteen minutes per half hour.

Second, because there are a maximum of three readers, it is far more likely that each is attending to what the others are reading—and much easier for you to tell when they aren't. If your readers are not engaged, it is easy to redirect them or give them a break by briefly discussing the selection, before picking up your reading again. And third, the students are not performing unrehearsed

material in front of their class. Instead, they are reading aloud in
a supportive atmosphere that is conducive to practice and where
assistance is readily available—in front of you and possibly a class-
mate with similar reading difficulties. If you choose to read with
your students in this manner, it is worth again stressing that each
student have a copy of the material you are reading.

Because you have flexibility when you are working one-on-one
or with pairs, you can also choose appropriate strategies based on
both your student's needs and the nature of the text. For example,
choral reading might be best for poems and echo reading might be a
good choice for particularly challenging texts. If, on the other hand,
you are working with a large classroom that has only one or two disfluent readers, you are unlikely to have the luxury of spending thirty
to sixty minutes working on strategies to make the text accessible for
them. As such, it is likely that you will want to rely on some of the
following approaches to help develop those readers' fluency within
the format of your broader literacy curriculum, possibly as part of
your literacy centers or your students' independent reading time.

Repeated Readings

Perhaps the best-known fluency strategy is repeated readings. Often
referred to as an unassisted approach (Dowhower, 1989), it does not
incorporate the use of a model, relying instead on the student's use
of repetition as the basis for independent practice. The approach
was developed as an alternative to the common practice of having
students read new material each day to improve their word recognition skills (Dahl, 1974; Samuels, 1979). Jay Samuels and Patricia Dahl
felt that, if students could instead increase the amount of practice
they completed on a given passage, they might experience greater
success developing their automaticity. The authors further believed
that these improvements in reading fluency would occur, not only

on the practiced material, but also on previously unread texts. In other words, when students encountered the words they had practiced in a new passage, they would be identified more quickly there as well. Since its initial conception, the effectiveness of repeated readings to develop students' accuracy, automaticity, prosody and comprehension has been demonstrated across numerous studies (see Dowhower, 1989).

The repeated readings procedure is quite straightforward—which makes it relatively easy to implement. There is one caveat, however: because you need to assess the students over the course of several readings, it can be difficult to use this strategy with large numbers of students. In fact, its design renders it most effective when used with one student at a time. The primary aim of this approach is to increase the automaticity of students whose decoding is accurate but deliberate. These students are likely to be exceedingly slow readers, even when the words they are encountering are common and should already be established as part of their **sight vocabulary**—the words an individual can recognize automatically, without relying on analysis for identification.

Repeated readings has two basic components. As with the majority of the procedures recommended in this book, the first step involves selecting a text that the student finds interesting and that is challenging. The second step involves recording both the number of **words** read **per minute (wpm)** and any miscues the student makes on each reading of the passage (see Figure 5.1; e.g., Ash & Hagwood, 2000). This procedure allows students to track both the increase in the word-per-minute rate and the decrease in the number of miscues—a process that has been shown to be highly motivating for struggling readers (e.g., Kuhn & Schwanenflugel, 2006). The student is expected to reread a passage either a set number of times (usually between three and five) or until a predetermined number of correct words per minute and a corresponding number of miscues has been reached.[1]

Figure 5.1

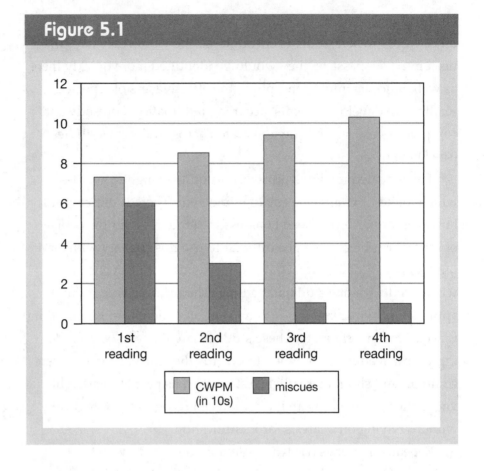

While repeated readings is clearly effective at improving students' word recognition, there has been a concern that, by asking students to focus on increasing their reading rate, the approach overemphasizes automaticity at the expense of comprehension (e.g., O'Shea, Sindelar, & O'Shea, 1985, 1987; Kuhn, 2005). In order to determine whether it is possible for struggling readers to focus on improving their reading rate while maintaining their comprehension, Lawrence O'Shea, Paul Sindelar, and Dorothy O'Shea conducted a repeated readings study in which they asked struggling readers to focus either on increasing their reading speed or on the meaning of the passage. What they found was that, whether students were asked to focus on speed or meaning, both groups increased their reading rate over the course of the repetitions; however, those students who were asked to read for meaning also demonstrated a better understanding of the text than did their peers. Given these findings, it is critical that you remind your students to focus on the meaning of a passage as well as on improving their rate when you ask them to use a repeated readings approach. This can be accomplished simply by asking them to remember what the passage was about before they begin reading.

Not only is repeated readings easily the most commonly used approach to fluency development, it has also proven highly effective over the course of numerous interventions (e.g., Dowhower, 1989). In addition, students who participated in repeated reading interventions have found the procedure to be highly motivating, allowing them to track the gains they make over the course of several rereadings. As a result, they can actually see themselves making progress over relatively short periods of time. Since motivation is critical in developing students' desire to read, repeated readings can help to create confidence in your learners' reading ability as well.

Lesson Snapshot

The procedure follows this outline:

- Identify an appropriately challenging text for your student and select a short passage from it (one hundred to two hundred words).[2] The number of words is set between one and two hundred both for ease of repetition (too long and the student may get fatigued by the process) and for ease of calculation!

- Provide both yourself and your student with a copy of the selection so that the student can read from his or her own text and you can note your student's rate and miscues on your copy.

continued

- Have your student read the text aloud without any support. Time this initial reading with a stopwatch to determine the number of words read per minute, and record any miscues on your copy of the text. Then transfer the wpm and number of miscues onto a chart such as the one in Figure 5.1. There should be an accuracy rating of between 85 and 90 percent on the initial reading. Any rating outside of this parameter will likely be either too challenging or not challenging enough for your student. Bear in mind that these guidelines may vary with each learner you work with and that you will need to make judgments based on both their ability and their responsiveness to the approach.

- After the initial reading, discuss the reading rate with your students and review any miscues as well. You should also discuss your goals for the passage with your students so that they understand why they will be rereading the passage and what they are aiming for with each additional reading of the text. In other words, establish a goal for their final wpm rate based on where they started and where you would like them to be after a set number of rereadings (because the bulk of the gains for repeated readings occurs between three and five readings, I suggest a maximum of five repetitions) and a miscue rate of 98 percent or higher (the independent level). Tell the students that you will be asking them what the passage is about so they do not end up overly focused on word recognition and speed; this is especially important if you use a selection that has not previously been read in its entirety.

- Have your student review the passage silently before rereading it out loud for a second time; although this step is not necessary, some students find the procedure increases their comfort level with the text.

- Next, have your student reread the passage while you record the new words per minute rate along with the change in the number of miscues.

- The student should continue rereading the passage (up to five times) until the predetermined rate and number of miscues (one or two per one hundred words) have been reached. You may find that your student experiences greater success when you divide the rereadings into two or three sessions, because this allows the reader to gain familiarity with the text.

- Several things are important to bear in mind regarding this process:

  - First, it is essential that you emphasize increasing your students' reading rate on these passages since your primary goal is to help them establish automatic word recognition.

  - A learner's independent reading level is considered to be a 98 percent accuracy rate. As such, it is important to remember that if the students make one or two miscues per one hundred words, they are reading as well as a skilled reader. Should you insist on word-perfect reading, you may end up slowing down your students' reading. Since the goal of this activity is to increase automaticity, such an insistence could prove counterproductive.

  - Similarly, you may find that your student repeatedly miscues the same one or two words in every rereading. If so, simply point out the correct pronunciation of the word when the reading is finished. This happens often, and it is best not to overemphasize the miscue by insisting on word-perfect reading because the incorrect pronunciation may end up further engrained in the student's memory.

  - Finally, if your student is unable to achieve the set criteria in five repetitions, it may be because the text is too difficult. If that is the case, you should move to an easier passage, one with a lower number of miscues on the initial reading, and build from there. On the other hand, if the learner is an exceedingly slow reader, you may be expecting too great

continued

an increase in their speed in just a few sessions. Look over the data for reading rate provided in Table 2.1 (page 31) and determine a criterion rate that you think is reasonable given the student's current reading development.

- Once your student has reached the desired reading rate and number of miscues on a given selection, have the student read another passage at the same reading level (this can either be another section taken from the same text or from another text at the same reading level). Continue this process until your student can read a selection at that level relatively fluently on the initial attempt, at which point you can begin to select passages from material that is at a slightly more difficult reading level.

Neurological Impress Method (NIM)

The next approach, the neurological impress method (NIM), was devised by R. G. Heckelman (1969, 1986) as a way of assisting struggling readers in their attempts to become fluent. Although the original design seems a bit antiquated—the student sits in front of the teacher while the teacher speaks into the student's ear as they read in unison from the same book—the approach was effective. The method was meant to impress the words on the learner's brain by speaking directly into the ear, but its actual effectiveness is likely to have resulted from reading in unison while tracking the text and providing support rather than any special positioning of voice to ear on the part of the skilled reader! The strategy also involves having the teacher vary the pace of the reading, so that sometimes it is faster or slower or louder or softer. The unison reading continues until the teacher notices that the student is starting to tire. Looking at this approach from our current vantage point, we can see that several aspects of the NIM method are critical to fluency development, including the support provided by having a skilled reader serve as a model, the practice that occurs through engaging in extensive supported reading, having the student track the text as it is being read in order to reinforce the connection between oral and written language, and the emphasis on prosodic elements that the skilled reader provides through the varied and expressive rendition of texts.

As your student becomes more capable of reading material at a given level, move on to more challenging text, and encourage your student to continue reading material written at the previous reading level on his or her own. This can be particularly effective if you are working with series books from a series such as *Clifford the Big Red Dog* (Bridwell, 1997), *Curious George* (Rey, 1973), *Kristy's Great Idea* (from the Baby-Sitters Club series) (Martin, 1995), or *The Bartimaeus Trilogy* (Stroud, 2006). The repetition of key words across books will help the learners read these texts independently, allowing you to move on to material at a higher reading level for your instructional selections.

Lesson Snapshot

This is a straightforward, easy-to-implement method, especially when working one-on-one with a student:

- Begin by selecting a text that the student is interested in and that is somewhat challenging. This is a great opportunity to pick a book that the learner wants to read, but can't read alone. For example, when series books from The Magic Treehouse, Lemony Snicket, or the Warriors series catch on, struggling readers often want to read what their peers are reading, but can't read them independently. Reading such material allows learners to feel like they are part of the larger literacy community.

continued

- Sit side by side with your student—each with your own copy of the text you are reading. I cannot stress enough how essential it is that each of you have your own copy whenever you are reading with, rather than to, a student. This not only allows your students to follow along with the reading but also helps them solidify their knowledge of the speech-print connection and feel ownership of the method, an understanding that is critical to their further reading development.

- Begin your **unison**, or choral, **reading** with your student at a normal rate; in other words, do not slow down your reading to meet your student's pace. Instead, encourage students to pick up their reading rate, forcing them to keep up with the rhythm of an expressive rendering of the text. If they are unable to keep pace with you, it is okay to slow down a bit, but not so much that the phrasing becomes awkward or you fall into word-by-word reading. If students are still unable to keep up with your pacing, it may be best to select a text that is somewhat closer to their instructional or independent level.

- It is also important that you vary your reading pace, expression, and volume as a way of helping your student become accustom to different interpretations of a selection through a focus on a range of prosodic elements.

- Although you must keep an eye out for signs that your student is becoming fatigued, try initially to read from the same text for at least five minutes and build from there. Struggling readers have to develop their stamina for reading; by working with a partner in a scaffolded manner, you are ensuring that this will occur.

Reading-While-Listening

Reading-while-listening was developed by Carol Chomsky (1976) as a way of assisting students who have solid decoding skills but are having difficulty transferring this knowledge to the reading of connected text. The strategy was designed specifically as a way to help five third graders who were experiencing a great deal of difficultly with their reading development. Despite extensive instruction in word recognition strategies and success at identifying words in isolation, they seemed unable to apply what they knew to their reading. As a result, these learners were not only reading one to two years below grade level but also claimed to intensely dislike reading. Rather than providing them with additional decoding instruction, an approach that had not worked to that point, Chomsky felt it might be more effective to expose these children to significant amounts of connected text in an accessible format. To test this theory, she created tape-recordings of two dozen books that ranged in reading level from second to fifth grade and that were considered too challenging for the students to read on their own. The procedure asked students to listen repeatedly to the recordings as they read along in the text and continued with a given selection until they were able to read the material fluently. The children could choose what they were going to read from among the available tapes and could also determine their own pace for reading them.

The process started slowly, with learners having difficulty coordinating their eye movements with the voices on tape. Eventually, with practice, it became easier to listen to the narration while keeping track of the text. This allowed them to read a particular selection until they were able to provide a fluent, independent rendition of it, at which point they moved on to the next book. Another important aspect of this process was the role the practice had in the students' overall fluency development; that is, it took the students less time to reach mastery on each subsequent selection, indicating that they were not only improving their word recognition and reading rate on the stories they were practicing but also able to transfer these gains to previously unread passages. Even more telling was the anecdotal evidence that parents and teachers shared; according to these adults, the children involved in this process were far more willing to read independently and to engage in writing activities than prior to the intervention. As such, the procedure can be seen as one that assists learners in becoming engaged readers—readers who are likely to enjoy reading a text on their own, either for pleasure or for information.

Carol Chomsky originally designed this procedure as a fairly independent one; students were even responsible for determining the length and frequency of their sessions. However, you may feel more comfortable setting a time frame for your learners to work with their recordings; for example, asking them to read along with a book-on-tape during your independent reading period or as part of a center. The procedure also requires less direct monitoring on your part than does the traditional repeated reading method. As a result, there is often a concern that the technique can turn into a listening lesson rather than a reading lesson, with little active reading engagement on the part of the learners. Despite this concern, the research indicates that your students will actively participate in the process as long as they are held accountable for their reading, either through the completion of a running record at the end of a selection or simply by having your students read the text to you on a regular basis, say once a week. Not only do students appear to enjoy the taped stories but they also display pride in their growing reading ability and their success with the texts.

This procedure is a bit more time-consuming in terms of organization than many of the others discussed in this chapter, but it is possible to buy unabridged versions of many books-on-tape, which can lessen the amount of time it takes to prepare the recordings. Moreover, although this approach was designed for individual learners, Paul Hollingsworth (1978) has had success using recordings (a variation of the NIM procedure) with a number of students at the same time by using an adaptor that allows several students to listen to the same selection simultaneously. As long as the students are reading along as they listen to the story and the pacing and challenge level are appropriate, this modification has the potential to be used either with a flexible group or in a center with more than one student at a time.

Lesson Snapshot

- In order to begin this procedure, you need to record or purchase narrated versions of a range of materials for your struggling readers. As mentioned, it is critical, if you are buying books on tape, that they be unabridged. It is also possible to get volunteers to create these recordings for you, but if you do so, make sure that the narrators read not only smoothly but also expressively, since their renderings of the text serve as models for your struggling readers. It is also worth considering alternatives to tape recordings, such as CDs or podcasts, as cassette recorders begin to be phased out.

- It is important to have a variety of recorded materials available for students to use. Assess students' reading levels and include texts at the top end of their instructional levels as well as texts that are several levels above their instructional levels. For example, in the original study, students were reading anywhere from the first- through the second-grade reading levels, yet the texts ranged from the second- to the fifth-grade reading levels—quite a span for students to select

continued

from. Next, have books with short chapters (e.g., *The Golly Sisters Go West*) as well as books with longer chapters (e.g., *Bunnicula*) and books that have a continuous text without chapter breaks (e.g., *The Snowy Day*); this allows readers to select the amount of text that they will be accountable for at a given time and lets them work at their own comfort level.

- In terms of actual procedure, explain to your students that they are not just listening to the story, but need to read along with the narration in order to improve their own reading. This will take a number of repetitions, and students may initially want to mumble or whisper read along with the recording in order to keep their place, possibly into "phones" made out of PVC pipes to minimize the noise. It is a good idea to have them shift to silent reading as they become more familiar with the process since this is your ultimate goal for them.

- When students feel ready to read the text without the support of the recording, ask them to read for you. You can either take a running record of their reading or simply listen to their oral reading to judge how fluent they have become with the material (using an inventory such as the NAEP in Table 2.2 could help you with your evaluation). If you think that the students are reasonably fluent with their text, ask them either to continue reading their selection (e.g., the next chapter) or, if you feel the selection is no longer challenging enough, to move on to more difficult material and complete their current selection independently. On the other hand, if they are still disfluent with their current text, ask them to continue to practice with that selection, or move to an easier text.

Cross-Age Reading

A common problem among older struggling readers is that they do not want to be seen reading texts they consider to be babyish, even though they often need practice using material written for early readers. An effective solution to this dilemma was developed by Linda Labbo and Bill Teale (1990). They created the cross-age reading strategy to give such readers an alternative purpose for reading texts written for young learners; they asked struggling fifth graders to read to kindergarten students from books that the younger students were likely to enjoy. This gave the older learners practice reading relatively easy books without looking as though they were doing so simply to improve their own reading. Instead, they believed they were preparing these texts in order to perform for a younger audience. The struggling readers prepared for their read-alouds in three ways. First, they were taught to select texts that their audience would enjoy; second, they practiced reading their selection until they were able to read it smoothly and with expression; and third, they were taught a number of ways to engage the kindergartners in discussions of the books. Significantly, the procedure helped several of the cross-age readers "to break poor oral reading habits" (Labbo & Teale, 1990, p. 365). It also helped these students make significant gains on a standardized reading measure when compared to students who either participated in an art project with the kindergartners or simply continued working with their basal readers. And, according to the authors and the teachers, both the fifth graders and the kindergartners enjoyed these story sessions. All of these results demonstrate the project's success.

Although this procedure is effective as is, it could also be modified so that the students create recordings of their readings rather than simply perform them for an audience. These recordings could be completed either in addition to reading to younger students, or as an alternative to these performances. Similarly, the recordings themselves could either be placed in listening centers for the youngest students or be used as resources for the reading-while-listening approach discussed earlier.

Lesson Snapshot

Although, the cross-age reading procedure was used with several struggling readers at once, students worked independently on their texts, hence its inclusion in this chapter. In order for your student or students to participate in such a project, you need to follow a three-step process:

- First, help your students select texts that younger learners (e.g., kindergartners or first or second graders) will enjoy and that are challenging, but not too challenging, for your older readers. Depending on their current reading levels, these could be a relatively simple chapter book, such as *Frog and Toad Are Friends* (Lobel, 1970), or a more complex picture book, such as *Stellaluna* (Cannon, 1999).

- Second, the students should practice reading the book until they are able to read it with expression and without hesitation. Since the students will likely be practicing the text on their own, their selection should be closer to their independent level than is the case for most of the strategies recommended in this book; that is, somewhere around a 95 percent accuracy level on the initial reading. Of course, you can vary this based on their success with a particular selection, and you should select increasingly challenging texts as your students' reading ability continues to improve.

- Third, show your students how to interact with their audience by asking questions that will require the listeners to think about the readings. For example, simply showing your readers how to pick appropriate stopping places in order to ask what might happen next will help develop listener engagement with the text. At the same time, it will help your readers develop a comprehension strategy that, if transferred to their own reading, could benefit their own understanding of texts as well.

Conducting Effective Fluency Instruction for Pairs and Individuals—Some Final Thoughts

With the range of reading abilities found in most classrooms, it is likely that at least some of your students will benefit from fluency instruction. If you are lucky enough to be able to provide these students with one-on-one tutoring or can work with pairs of students, either as a teacher or as a reading specialist, then partner reading, repeated reading, or the NIM approach are all viable options. However, if this simply isn't feasible in your current classroom structure, you may want to integrate reading-while-listening or cross-aged reading into your literacy centers or your independent reading time; by providing these options for all your students rather than just your struggling readers, you are minimizing the likelihood that these activities will stigmatize your disfluent readers. You may even find that one of your older struggling readers could act as a tutor for younger schoolmates and that both could benefit from the time spent reading together.

Study Guide Questions

- Think about the students in your class (or the students you are working with in a tutoring situation) and identify those students who would benefit from fluency instruction. Which of the strategies presented in this chapter would most benefit these students?

- How could you integrate some of the strategies presented in this chapter into your literacy centers? What materials would you need to make these approaches work for your students?

- How could you integrate some of the strategies presented in this chapter into your tutoring? Think about your tutoring sessions; how would you need to rework your current activities to include a fluency component in your instruction?

- Select one student that you feel would benefit from one (or several) of these instructional approaches. What strategy would you use? What text would you select? What do you feel would be the right level of challenge for this student? Remember that material used for fluency instruction should be more challenging than material that is at the student's instructional level because of the additional support provided through various types of scaffolding.

Notes

1. Both a set number of readings (up to seven) and a predetermined rate have been used as the criteria for determining whether a student has achieved mastery on a given passage. However, the greatest amount of growth occurs between the third and the fifth repetition (depending on the text difficulty and the learner's ability). Therefore, if your students have not reached their criteria by the fifth reading, you should consider using an easier selection.

2. Since you are using selections for instruction and not assessment, you may want to use texts that have previously been read in their entirety to prevent your students from viewing this activity exclusively as an exercise in word identification and speed.

Chapter 6

Approaches to Supplement Your Literacy Curriculum

Instructional Approach	Grade Levels	Grouping	Type of Text
Paired Repeated Reading	• Originally grade 3 • Can be used with grades 2 and above	• Supplement for whole-class instruction • Supplement for small-group instruction	Challenging or instructional level texts
Fluency Development Lesson	• Any grade level above first grade	• Supplement for whole-class instruction • Supplement for small-group instruction	Brief, challenging texts (50–150 words)
Reader's Theater	• Any grade level above first grade	• Supplement for whole-class instruction • Supplement for small-group instruction	Challenging texts

■ Is there a benefit to integrating supplemental fluency approaches into an existing literacy curriculum?

■ What approaches can be used on a supplementary basis with your primary texts?

■ What methods can be used as occasional alternatives to your primary texts?

How Can Fluency Instruction Supplement My Literacy Curriculum?

Throughout this book, I have presented approaches that use different instructional configurations in order to meet your students' needs. If you have a class of students who are fairly fluent readers, you may simply want to supplement your current literacy instruction to further enhance their reading ability. Or you may want to use a strategy on an occasional basis to ensure that your students are continuing to develop their reading fluency. The methods presented in this chapter can be used to complement your current literacy curriculum with effective approaches to fluency instruction.

Paired Repeated Readings

The first supplemental approach is based on a modification of the repeated readings strategy that has proven to be so effective as a means of improving reading fluency. Although repeated readings has been shown to be a valuable aid to fluency development across numerous studies, it can be difficult to implement with more than one or two students because it relies so heavily on the teacher to provide feedback and record the changes in the learner's reading. To counter this difficulty, Patricia Koskinen and Irene Blum (1984, 1986) designed paired repeated readings for use with groups of students. Since most teachers have little, if any, time on an average day to provide their learners with individual instruction, the authors believed that paired repeated readings would allow students to work with one another to improve their reading fluency, thereby taking some of the onus off the teacher.

The original intervention was implemented with below-average third-grade readers using grade-level material. The authors found that the students who used the paired repeated readings approach significantly outperformed their peers who worked on study activities instead; they also made significantly fewer meaning-changing miscues. This method seems also to have many of the benefits of the original repeated readings procedure: (1) rereading a given passage in this manner not only improves automaticity, but reading fluency in general; (2) since this method has a built-in audience for the reader, it is easy to incorporate expression into the criteria measures; and (3) it is likely that the improvements in the practiced passages will transfer to previously unread material in a manner similar to that of the original repeated readings procedure and other similar fluency approaches.

While paired repeated readings have a focus on improving rate and accuracy through practice, the role of the listener also ensures that there is a strong emphasis on the prosodic elements of the text, such as appropriate phrasing and expression. You can integrate this approach into your lesson plans using virtually any text that you are reading with your students, including basal readers or the content-area texts that are often a challenge to many learners. Because paired repeated readings is designed as a supplement to the literacy curriculum, it is possible to use this strategy with the entire class. But you can also use this procedure with your flexible reading groups by allowing students in one group to take part in the procedure while you are working with one of the other groups.

Lesson Snapshot

■ Since your students will be working with a partner, when you first introduce this practice, it is essential to demonstrate how they should read with one another; this includes discussing and modeling how to use the appropriate volume when sitting next to one another (in other words, using

continued

their quiet—or inside—voices rather than their noisy—or outdoor—voices!).

- Explain ways in which your students can provide one another with positive feedback. This teaches students how to act as a coach for each other, ensuring that their comments are positive and contribute to their partner's improvement. Comments can include, "you were able to read more quickly the second time through," or "you sounded more excited when you were reading this time." You can also ask your class to generate their own ideas for positive feedback and leave these on a chart so that models of what to say are readily available.

- After completing an initial reading and discussion of a story or content-area text with your class, ask your students to break into pairs. You can select partners for your students or they can self-select their pairs (see the section on partner reading in Chapter 1 for an effective partnering procedure).

- Determine which student will read aloud first; you may want to create a schedule in which the students alternate who goes first in order to minimize disputes between pairs.

- Students then select a passage that is approximately fifty words long from their reading material. As the authors suggest, stress that each student in the pair select a different passage in order to prevent them from directly comparing their reading to one another.

- The first step in the actual procedure is to have the students read through their passages silently.

- Each student then takes a turn reading through the passage three times aloud. After each rendition, the student evaluates her reading of the passage, recording how well her turns went and noting any improvements in a notebook or on a self-evaluation sheet.

- The partner's role is to listen carefully to the reader and to provide the reader with positive feedback. However, the listener should comment only on the second and third readings, identifying improvements that the reader has made and noting these positive changes on a listening sheet.

- For the final step, the pair switches roles and repeats the process.

Fluency Development Lesson

The Fluency Development Lesson (FDL) (Rasinski et al., 1994) was also designed as a strategy that could be implemented in conjunction with a teacher's regular reading curriculum. It consists of fifteen minutes of daily instruction and involves the shared reading of a fifty- to one hundred-fifty-word text. This approach integrates Tim Rasinski's fluency principles (modeling, support, opportunities for practice, and a focus on phrasing; see Chapter 1 for a full discussion of these principles) in a brief and easy-to-implement format. The teacher begins with an initial reading of the text while the students follow along in their own copy. This is followed by a short discussion of the material and several whole-class choral readings (see Chapter 1 for a discussion of choral reading). In the next step, the students break into pairs. As with the paired repeated readings approach, each partner practices reading the text aloud three times (see Chapter 1 for an explanation of partner reading and ways of partnering your students). During this phase, as one student takes a turn reading the text, the second listens and provides supportive feedback. On completion of the first student's turn, the pair exchange roles. For the final in-class activity, students can volunteer to perform the passage for their peers. Encourage the entire class to practice reading the selection at home as well. Overall, the approach creates a cohesive daily routine that can be integrated into virtually any literacy curriculum.

In the original study, the fifteen-minute lesson plan was used every day for six months with a group of twenty-eight second graders (Rasinski et al., 1994). In order to evaluate the treatment's effectiveness, the designers looked at the reading development of students who used the FDL approach alongside that of another group of twenty-seven students. The second group of learners took part in a broad range of reading activities over the same period, but the use of repetition in their class was kept to a minimum. The results from pre- and post-testing on an informal reading inventory indicated that the students participating in the FDL made significant gains in reading rate (their rates at the end of the intervention were between 81.7 percent and 93.6 percent higher than their initial reading rate) when compared to the students in the non-FDL (their gains were much lower, ranging between 34.2 and 49.2 percent). Given the importance of automaticity in fluency development, these results suggest that FDL can be a useful tool in your overall literacy curriculum.

Because FDL procedure involves the use of a short text (50 to 150 words) as the basis of your fluency instruction, the daily fifteen-minute lesson plan can be incorporated into your existing curriculum relatively easily. Thankfully, an abundance of material written for primary grade readers falls into this word range. Such material could also be used with older struggling readers, but older students may be more receptive to the use of poems, excerpts from speeches, short passages from stories, or brief sections from nonfiction texts. Because they are less likely to feel uncomfortable with such material, they are more likely to benefit from these selections as well. A third option is to use a short passage from a longer text that you have been discussing as part of a shared reading, whether this is a piece of literature, a selection from a history or science text, or any other piece you feel is appropriate for multiple readings.

Given the length of many literacy periods at present and the relative ease of implementing this approach, many teachers have found the FDL to be a useful supplement to a literacy curriculum. Despite (or sometimes because of) a host of initiatives and mandates, learners still have insufficient opportunities to practice their reading; the FDL provides them with the chance to read both repeatedly and widely. Such access to text can only assist learners in becoming better readers.

Lesson Snapshot

- After selecting an appropriately challenging short text for your class, read it to your students, modeling both appropriate expression and phrasing. Make sure that your class is following along in their own copies of the passage by circulating around the room.

- Next, discuss the text with your class. Since there is a good chance that at least some of your selections will be poems or speeches, this is a particularly important step, both to promote understanding of the material and in terms of the students' later interpretation of the selections. Remember, though, that these are short passages, and the entire lesson should be completed in fifteen minutes, so lengthy discussions are not necessary and may become unwieldy. If the text is part of a broader lesson, a brief review of the selection may suffice.

- Following the discussion, have your students break into pairs and practice reading the text three times. As one student

continued

takes a turn reading, the other student is responsible for listening. The student listening also provides the reader with positive feedback regarding her oral rendering of the passage (see Chapter 1 for an explanation of effective partnering practices and the paired repeated readings for a discussion of ways to ensure positive feedback). After the first partner completes three readings, the students switch roles and the listener takes a turn reading the text.

- On completing their practice, the students can volunteer to perform the selection to the class.
- Encourage your students to take the selection home for additional practice.

Reader's Theater

Reader's theater is another supplemental approach that is enjoyed by virtually every group of students who have used it (Allington, 2001; Bidwell, 1990; Henning, 1974). It is also very effective in giving your learners a real purpose for repeatedly reading their material, and very flexible: you can use it with virtually any reading material, including poetry and nonfiction (Hoyt, 2000). But no matter how enjoyable reader's theater is, remember that it is a supplemental approach and should not take over your entire literacy curriculum (something I have seen happen as the result of students' positive response to the procedure). Use it instead to infuse some spice into your curriculum rather than as the main ingredient.

In terms of reading material, you can either choose ready-made selections—for example, plays or poems for multiple voices—or rewrite a text or a portion of a text, as a play-like performance piece. Plays or poems for multiple voices are usually available in your literature anthologies or basal readers. Alternatively, there are often collections of these works in your school or public library. If you decide to rewrite a text, you don't need to turn it into a play per se; instead, you could rewrite it as a third-person narration in several parts or as an **antiphonal reading** (a version of choral reading in which students take turns reading from a text). You could also have older students or your more skilled readers rewrite a text as a reader's theater piece thereby providing these learners with extra literacy practice. Reader's theater differs from a traditional play insofar as it is designed for casual performances; there is no need for props, sets, costumes, or even the memorization of lines! Rather, students use expression to bring the text to life by relying on their voices and by keeping in mind the various ways the text can be interpreted as they are practicing it.

As with other fluency approaches, reader's theater helps develop automatic word recognition; it also places a strong emphasis on the use of appropriate expression to convey the text's meaning. Because of its flexibility, reader's theater can easily be applied as a supplemental activity, either for smaller groups of learners or for the class as whole. Since students work with their peers throughout this procedure, your skilled readers have the opportunity to act as models for your struggling readers, and, if reading chorally, can help these students with pronunciation, expression, and pace. Further, since the students have ample opportunity to practice their parts, this approach is especially helpful for students having the greatest difficulty integrating their word recognition, phrasing, and expression into a prosodic rendering of text. However, this benefit comes with a caveat: it is critical that your struggling readers are given parts that are of reasonable length. Since these students are most in need of practice, they are unlikely to develop their fluency if assigned too brief a role, and would actually be better off working on a different fluency-oriented reading activity.

Lesson Snapshot

- Begin this procedure by selecting a play or poem that the students will enjoy practicing or by adapting material that lends itself to being performed aloud.

- Since you want a selection that is worthy of multiple readings, it should be somewhat challenging for the majority of your learners. Because of this, you will likely need to read the selection to the students prior to their attempting it on their own. As is the case with other strategies presented throughout this book, when you are introducing your class to challenging material, you may want to read it to them as they follow along in their own copy, or you may want them to echo or choral read along with you, or you may want to do both, depending on the overall difficulty of the passage (see Chapter 1 for a discussion of choral and echo reading).

- After completing your initial reading, divide the students into groups. There are several options depending on whether you want your students to work on a single text or whether you want them to use multiple texts. You can either have several groups reading different selections, or have one performance completed by the whole class. In the first case, you could use the process as an activity for flexible groups by selecting several different texts; this would allow each group to perform a unique piece and prevent any comparison among your students. If you choose to use different material for different groups, make sure that each group's text is sufficiently challenging, otherwise you may find the material is ineffective as an aid for fluency development. Alternatively, you could give several students the same role and have them perform their parts chorally.

- Once the mechanics of the process are determined, provide the students with sufficient time to practice their parts.

Have the students read their passage(s) both silently and aloud—either individually or as a chorus. They should also be given the opportunity to offer and receive positive feedback from their fellow performers in order to improve on their rendition.

- When your students feel comfortable with the material and can read the piece fluently, they should perform their theatrical interpretation of the selection for their fellow classmates or another available audience.

- Students can further benefit from the introduction of opportunities for self-evaluation and the positive feedback of their peers.

General Fluency Approaches— Revisited

It is worth briefly revisiting three strategies that can be used whenever you encounter text that is too challenging for your students to read on their own: echo, choral, and partner reading. Although they are the backbone of a number of the more structured strategies described throughout this book (see Chapter 1 for a more detailed description of the procedures), they can simply be integrated into your lesson plans whenever you encounter text that requires support since they do not need substantial planning to be effective (Meisinger & Bradley, 2007). They are the easiest way to begin the transition from ineffective oral reading instruction to instruction that actually fosters fluency development. Echo reading provides the most scaffolding, whereas partner reading provides the least, and choral reading falls in between the two. The types of texts that these approaches are most compatible with varies, too. Echo reading can be used as a way of providing learners with access to challenging text, but would not be a good choice for material students can already read independently or with minimal support. Choral reading, on the other hand, is best for shorter texts, such as poems, or to reread a longer selection to confirm pacing, use of expression, word identification, and appropriate phrasing. The third approach, partner reading, works well either with instructional level texts that have not been previously practiced or for an independent reading of challenging material that has already been covered with the support of a skilled reader. Asking children to partner read a challenging text that has not been practiced in a supported manner is likely to lead to frustration and a dislike of the task at hand. Given that these approaches can be used with any type of grouping, from whole class to one-on-one instruction, with no preparation means that they are immediate and effective alternatives to round-robin reading.

Conclusions

Since fluency instruction is being integrated into the classroom with greater frequency, it is essential that you have a clear understanding not only of what it is and which of your students can benefit from it but also of how to effectively teach and assess it. The information presented throughout this text offers many strategies that are easy to implement and highly effective. By integrating your knowledge of fluency instruction into the classroom, you will be better able to assist your students as they develop into skilled readers who are prepared for the challenges they face both from academic texts and from texts they encounter in their homes, their communities, and, ultimately, their work. By establishing such an environment, you will truly be helping your learners reach a brighter future.

- What is the value of using supplemental approaches to fluency instruction?

- How would you use the paired repeated reading strategy with your students? Is it something you would implement as part of a shared reading lesson or your flexible grouping? How would you partner the students in your class or in your groups?

- Under what circumstances would you use the Fluency Development Lesson, as a regular introduction to your literacy lessons or as an occasional strategy to be used with specific types of texts, such as poetry? Can you identify any specific examples from your literature anthology, basal reader, or other material (e.g., from the Internet, a weekly classroom magazine, or a trade book) that you would use for the Fluency Development Lesson with your class? How would you design your lessons using this approach?

- Identify a text that you feel would be fun to read aloud in a dramatic way. How would you use it for a reader's theater lesson? Would you create a large number of individual parts or fewer parts for groups of students to read chorally? Would you use an already existing play or would you modify a narrative or expository text? If the latter, would you rewrite it yourself or would you have your students rewrite it? Would you use one text for the whole class or several selections for heterogeneous or homogeneous groups?

- Finally, think about the strategies presented across these chapters along with your overall literacy curriculum. What place does fluency instruction have within your classroom? Which students would benefit from such instruction? What will be your first concrete steps to make this shift in your instruction a reality?

Appendixes

Given the significance of challenging texts as a mainstay for the fluency approaches presented throughout this book, I feel it is important to provide a list of high-quality children's literature. These texts deal with essential themes and ideas and are worthy of the class time that you would dedicate to them should you choose to integrate them into your fluency instruction. They include the Newbery Medal and Honor Books, Caldecott Medal Winners and Honor Books, and the Coretta Scott King Book Award and Honor Books. While these lists are not all-inclusive, they certainly provide a useful place to start and are a valuable point of reference for any classroom teacher or literacy specialist. Additional resources can be found through the International Reading Association's website (www.reading.org), through books such as *The Fountas and Pinnell Leveled Book List, K–8* (Fountas & Pinnell, 2005) and *Best Books for Beginning Readers* (Gunning, 1998), and through series books such as the I Can Read texts for early readers published by HarperTrophy. While levels will vary as students become more skilled in their reading, remember that the scaffolding provided by fluency-oriented instruction is only effective if used to support reading that is challenging for students and will improve their word recognition, their reading rate, their prosody, and, ultimately, their vocabulary and comprehension.

Newbery Medal and Honor Books, 1922–2007

2007 Medal Winner
The Higher Power of Lucky by Susan Patron (Simon & Schuster/Richard Jackson)

Honor Books
Penny from Heaven by Jennifer L. Holm (Random House)
Hattie Big Sky by Kirby Larson (Delacorte Press)
Rules by Cynthia Lord (Scholastic)

2006 Medal Winner
Criss Cross by Lynne Rae Perkins (Greenwillow Books/HarperCollins)

Honor Books
Whittington by Alan W. Armstrong (Random House)
Hitler Youth: Growing up in Hitler's Shadow by Susan Campbell Bartoletti (Scholastic)

Princess Academy by Shannon Hale (Bloomsbury Children's Books)
Show Way by Jacqueline Woodson (G. P. Putnam's Sons)

2005 Medal Winner
Kira-Kira by Cynthia Kadohata (Atheneum Books for Young Readers/
Simon & Schuster)

Honor Books
Al Capone Does My Shirts by Gennifer Choldenko (G. P. Putnam's Sons/a
division of Penguin Young Readers Group)
*The Voice That Challenged a Nation: Marian Anderson and the Struggle for Equal
Rights* by Russell Freedman (Clarion Books/Houghton Mifflin)
Lizzie Bright and the Buckminster Boy by Gary D. Schmidt (Clarion Books/
Houghton Mifflin)

2004 Medal Winner
*The Tale of Despereaux: Being the Story of a Mouse, a Princess, Some Soup, and a
Spool of Thread* by Kate DiCamillo (Candlewick Press)

Honor Books
Olive's Ocean by Kevin Henkes (Greenwillow Books)
*An American Plague: The True and Terrifying Story of the Yellow Fever Epidemic
of 1793* by Jim Murphy (Clarion Books)

2003 Medal Winner
Crispin: The Cross of Lead by Avi (Hyperion Books for Children)

Honor Books
The House of the Scorpion by Nancy Farmer (Atheneum)
Pictures of Hollis Woods by Patricia Reilly Giff (Random House/Wendy
Lamb Books)
Hoot by Carl Hiaasen (Knopf)
A Corner of the Universe by Ann M. Martin (Scholastic)
Surviving the Applewhites by Stephanie S. Tolan (HarperCollins)

2002 Medal Winner
A Single Shard by Linda Sue Park (Clarion Books/Houghton Mifflin)

Honor Books
Everything on a Waffle by Polly Horvath (Farrar, Straus, and Giroux)
Carver: A Life in Poems by Marilyn Nelson (Front Street)

2001 Medal Winner
A Year down Yonder by Richard Peck (Dial)

Honor Books
Hope Was Here by Joan Bauer (G. P. Putnam's Sons)
Because of Winn-Dixie by Kate DiCamillo (Candlewick Press)
Joey Pigza Loses Control by Jack Gantos (Farrar, Straus, and Giroux)
The Wanderer by Sharon Creech (Joanna Cotler Books/HarperCollins)

2000 Medal Winner
Bud, Not Buddy by Christopher Paul Curtis (Delacorte)

Honor Books
Getting Near to Baby by Audrey Couloumbis (Putnam)
Our Only May Amelia by Jennifer L. Holm (HarperCollins)
26 Fairmount Avenue by Tomie dePaola (Putnam)

1999 Medal Winner
Holes by Louis Sachar (Frances Foster)

Honor Book
A Long Way from Chicago by Richard Peck (Dial)

1998 Medal Winner
Out of the Dust by Karen Hesse (Scholastic)

Honor Books
Ella Enchanted by Gail Carson Levine (HarperCollins)
Lily's Crossing by Patricia Reilly Giff (Delacorte)
Wringer by Jerry Spinelli (HarperCollins)

1997 Medal Winner
The View from Saturday by E. L. Konigsburg (Jean Karl/Atheneum)

Honor Books
A Girl Named Disaster by Nancy Farmer (Richard Jackson/Orchard Books)
The Moorchild by Eloise McGraw (Margaret McElderry/Simon & Schuster)
The Thief by Megan Whalen Turner (Greenwillow/Morrow)
Belle Prater's Boy by Ruth White (Farrar, Straus, and Giroux)

1996 Medal Winner
The Midwife's Apprentice by Karen Cushman (Clarion)

Honor Books
What Jamie Saw by Carolyn Coman (Front Street)
The Watsons Go to Birmingham: 1963 by Christopher Paul Curtis (Delacorte)
Yolonda's Genius by Carol Fenner (Margaret K. McElderry/Simon & Schuster)
The Great Fire by Jim Murphy (Scholastic)

1995 Medal Winner
Walk Two Moons by Sharon Creech (HarperCollins)

Honor Books
Catherine, Called Birdy by Karen Cushman (Clarion)
The Ear, the Eye, and the Arm by Nancy Farmer (Jackson/Orchard)

1994 Medal Winner
The Giver by Lois Lowry (Houghton)

Honor Books
Crazy Lady by Jane Leslie Conly (HarperCollins)

Dragon's Gate by Laurence Yep (HarperCollins)
Eleanor Roosevelt: A Life of Discovery by Russell Freedman (Clarion Books)

1993 Medal Winner
Missing May by Cynthia Rylant (Jackson/Orchard)

Honor Books
What Hearts by Bruce Brooks (A Laura Geringer Book, a HarperCollins
    imprint)
The Dark-Thirty: Southern Tales of the Supernatural by Patricia McKissack
    (Knopf)
Somewhere in the Darkness by Walter Dean Myers (Scholastic Hardcover)

1992 Medal Winner
Shiloh by Phyllis Reynolds Naylor (Atheneum)

Honor Books
Nothing But the Truth: A Documentary Novel by Avi (Jackson/Orchard)
The Wright Brothers: How They Invented the Airplane by Russell Freedman
    (Holiday House)

1991 Medal Winner
Maniac Magee by Jerry Spinelli (Little, Brown)

Honor Book
The True Confessions of Charlotte Doyle by Avi (Jackson/Orchard)

1990 Medal Winner
Number the Stars by Lois Lowry (Houghton)

Honor Books
Afternoon of the Elves by Janet Taylor Lisle (Jackson/Orchard)
Shabanu, Daughter of the Wind by Suzanne Fisher Staples (Knopf)
The Winter Room by Gary Paulsen (Jackson/Orchard)

1989 Medal Winner
Joyful Noise: Poems for Two Voices by Paul Fleischman (Harper)

Honor Books
In the Beginning: Creation Stories from Around the World by Virginia Hamilton
    (Harcourt)
Scorpions by Walter Dean Myers (Harper)

1988 Medal Winner
Lincoln: A Photobiography by Russell Freedman (Clarion)

Honor Books
After the Rain by Norma Fox Mazer (Morrow)
Hatchet by Gary Paulsen (Bradbury)

1987 Medal Winner
The Whipping Boy by Sid Fleischman (Greenwillow)

Honor Books
A Fine White Dust by Cynthia Rylant (Bradbury)
On My Honor by Marion Dane Bauer (Clarion)
Volcano: The Eruption and Healing of Mount St. Helens by Patricia Lauber
(Bradbury)

1986 Medal Winner
Sarah, Plain and Tall by Patricia MacLachlan (Harper)

Honor Books
Commodore Perry in the Land of the Shogun by Rhoda Blumberg (Lothrop)
Dogsong by Gary Paulsen (Bradbury)

1985 Medal Winner
The Hero and the Crown by Robin McKinley (Greenwillow)

Honor Books
Like Jake and Me by Mavis Jukes (Knopf)
The Moves Make the Man by Bruce Brooks (Harper)
One-Eyed Cat by Paula Fox (Bradbury)

1984 Medal Winner
Dear Mr. Henshaw by Beverly Cleary (Morrow)

Honor Books
The Sign of the Beaver by Elizabeth George Speare (Houghton)
A Solitary Blue by Cynthia Voigt (Atheneum)
Sugaring Time by Kathryn Lasky (Macmillan)
The Wish Giver: Three Tales of Coven Tree by Bill Brittain (Harper)

1983 Medal Winner
Dicey's Song by Cynthia Voigt (Atheneum)

Honor Books
The Blue Sword by Robin McKinley (Greenwillow)
Doctor De Soto by William Steig (Farrar)
Graven Images by Paul Fleischman (Harper)
Homesick: My Own Story by Jean Fritz (Putnam)
Sweet Whispers, Brother Rush by Virginia Hamilton (Philomel)

1982 Medal Winner
A Visit to William Blake's Inn: Poems for Innocent and Experienced Travelers by
Nancy Willard (Harcourt)

Honor Books
Ramona Quimby, Age 8 by Beverly Cleary (Morrow)
Upon the Head of the Goat: A Childhood in Hungary 1939–1944 by Aranka
Siegal (Farrar)

1981 Medal Winner
Jacob Have I Loved by Katherine Paterson (Crowell)

Honor Books
The Fledgling by Jane Langton (Harper)
A Ring of Endless Light by Madeleine L'Engle (Farrar)

1980 Medal Winner
A Gathering of Days: A New England Girl's Journal, 1830–1832 by Joan W. Blos
　　(Scribner)

Honor Book
The Road from Home: The Story of an Armenian Girl by David Kherdian
　　(Greenwillow)

1979 Medal Winner
The Westing Game by Ellen Raskin (Dutton)

Honor Book
The Great Gilly Hopkins by Katherine Paterson (Crowell)

1978 Medal Winner
Bridge to Terabithia by Katherine Paterson (Crowell)

Honor Books
Ramona and Her Father by Beverly Cleary (Morrow)
Anpao: An American Indian Odyssey by Jamake Highwater (Lippincott)

1977 Medal Winner
Roll of Thunder, Hear My Cry by Mildred D. Taylor (Dial)

Honor Books
Abel's Island by William Steig (Farrar)
A String in the Harp by Nancy Bond (Atheneum)

1976 Medal Winner
The Grey King by Susan Cooper (McElderry/Atheneum)

Honor Books
The Hundred Penny Box by Sharon Bell Mathis (Viking)
Dragonwings by Laurence Yep (Harper)

1975 Medal Winner
M. C. Higgins, the Great by Virginia Hamilton (Macmillan)

Honor Books
Figgs & Phantoms by Ellen Raskin (Dutton)
My Brother Sam Is Dead by James Lincoln Collier and Christopher Collier
　　(Four Winds)
The Perilous Gard by Elizabeth Marie Pope (Houghton)
Philip Hall Likes Me, I Reckon Maybe by Bette Greene (Dial)

1974 Medal Winner
The Slave Dancer by Paula Fox (Bradbury)

Honor Book
The Dark Is Rising by Susan Cooper (McElderry/Atheneum)

1973 Medal Winner
Julie of the Wolves by Jean Craighead George (Harper)
Honor Books
Frog and Toad Together by Arnold Lobel (Harper)
The Upstairs Room by Johanna Reiss (Crowell)
The Witches of Worm by Zilpha Keatley Snyder (Atheneum)

1972 Medal Winner
Mrs. Frisby and the Rats of NIMH by Robert C. O'Brien (Atheneum)
Honor Books
Incident at Hawk's Hill by Allan W. Eckert (Little, Brown)
The Planet of Junior Brown by Virginia Hamilton (Macmillan)
The Tombs of Atuan by Ursula K. Le Guin (Atheneum)
Annie and the Old One by Miska Miles (Little, Brown)
The Headless Cupid by Zilpha Keatley Snyder (Atheneum)

1971 Medal Winner
The Summer of the Swans by Betsy Byars (Viking)
Honor Books
Kneeknock Rise by Natalie Babbitt (Farrar)
Enchantress from the Stars by Sylvia Louise Engdahl (Atheneum)
Sing down the Moon by Scott O'Dell (Houghton)

1970 Medal Winner
Sounder by William H. Armstrong (Harper)
Honor Books
Our Eddie by Sulamith Ish-Kishor (Pantheon)
The Many Ways of Seeing: An Introduction to the Pleasures of Art by Janet
    Gaylord Moore (World)
Journey Outside by Mary Q. Steele (Viking)

1969 Medal Winner
The High King by Lloyd Alexander (Holt)
Honor Books
To Be a Slave by Julius Lester (Dial)
When Shlemiel Went to Warsaw and Other Stories by Isaac Bashevis Singer
    (Farrar)

1968 Medal Winner
From the Mixed-Up Files of Mrs. Basil E. Frankweiler by E. L. Konigsburg
    (Atheneum)

Honor Books
Jennifer, Hecate, Macbeth, William McKinley, and Me, Elizabeth by E. L.
    Konigsburg (Atheneum)
The Black Pearl by Scott O'Dell (Houghton)
The Fearsome Inn by Isaac Bashevis Singer (Scribner)
The Egypt Game by Zilpha Keatley Snyder (Atheneum)

1967 Medal Winner
Up a Road Slowly by Irene Hunt (Follett)

Honor Books
The King's Fifth by Scott O'Dell (Houghton)
Zlateh The Goat and Other Stories by Isaac Bashevis Singer (Harper)
The Jazz Man by Mary Hays Weik (Atheneum)

1966 Medal Winner
I, Juan de Pareja by Elizabeth Borton de Trevino (Farrar)

Honor Books
The Black Cauldron by Lloyd Alexander (Holt)
The Animal Family by Randall Jarrell (Pantheon)
The Noonday Friends by Mary Stolz (Harper)

1965 Medal Winner
Shadow of a Bull by Maia Wojciechowska (Atheneum)

Honor Book
Across Five Aprils by Irene Hunt (Follett)

1964 Medal Winner
It's Like This, Cat by Emily Neville (Harper)

Honor Books
Rascal: A Memoir of a Better Era by Sterling North (Dutton)
The Loner by Ester Wier (McKay)

1963 Medal Winner
A Wrinkle in Time by Madeleine L'Engle (Farrar)

Honor Books
Thistle and Thyme: Tales and Legends from Scotland by Sorche Nic Leodhas,
    pseud. (Leclaire Alger) (Holt)
Men of Athens by Olivia Coolidge (Houghton)

1962 Medal Winner
The Bronze Bow by Elizabeth George Speare (Houghton)

Honor Books
Frontier Living by Edwin Tunis (World)
The Golden Goblet by Eloise Jarvis McGraw (Coward)
Belling the Tiger by Mary Stolz (Harper)

1961 Medal Winner
Island of the Blue Dolphins by Scott O'Dell (Houghton)
Honor Books
America Moves Forward: A History for Peter by Gerald W. Johnson (Morrow)
Old Ramon by Jack Schaefer (Houghton)
The Cricket in Times Square by George Selden, pseud. (George Thompson) (Farrar)

1960 Medal Winner
Onion John by Joseph Krumgold (Crowell)
Honor Books
My Side of the Mountain by Jean Craighead George (Dutton)
America Is Born: A History for Peter by Gerald W. Johnson (Morrow)
The Gammage Cup by Carol Kendall (Harcourt)

1959 Medal Winner
The Witch of Blackbird Pond by Elizabeth George Speare (Houghton)
Honor Books
The Family under the Bridge by Natalie Savage Carlson (Harper)
Along Came a Dog by Meindert DeJong (Harper)
Chucaro: Wild Pony of the Pampa by Francis Kalnay (Harcourt)
The Perilous Road by William O. Steele (Harcourt)

1958 Medal Winner
Rifles for Watie by Harold Keith (Crowell)
Honor Books
The Horsecatcher by Mari Sandoz (Westminster)
Gone-Away Lake by Elizabeth Enright (Harcourt)
The Great Wheel by Robert Lawson (Viking)
Tom Paine, Freedom's Apostle by Leo Gurko (Crowell)

1957 Medal Winner
Miracles on Maple Hill by Virginia Sorensen (Harcourt)
Honor Books
Old Yeller by Fred Gipson (Harper)
The House of Sixty Fathers by Meindert DeJong (Harper)
Mr. Justice Holmes by Clara Ingram Judson (Follett)
The Corn Grows Ripe by Dorothy Rhoads (Viking)
Black Fox of Lorne by Marguerite de Angeli (Doubleday)

1956 Medal Winner
Carry On, Mr. Bowditch by Jean Lee Latham (Houghton)
Honor Books
The Secret River by Marjorie Kinnan Rawlings (Scribner)
The Golden Name Day by Jennie Lindquist (Harper)

Men, Microscopes, and Living Things by Katherine B. Shippen (Viking)

1955 Medal Winner
The Wheel on the School by Meindert DeJong (Harper)

Honor Books
The Courage of Sarah Noble by Alice Dalgliesh (Scribner)
Banner in the Sky by James Ullman (Lippincott)

1954 Medal Winner
. . . And Now Miguel by Joseph Krumgold (Crowell)

Honor Books
All Alone by Claire Huchet Bishop (Viking)
Shadrach by Meindert DeJong (Harper)
Hurry Home, Candy by Meindert DeJong (Harper)
Theodore Roosevelt, Fighting Patriot by Clara Ingram Judson (Follett)
Magic Maize by Mary and Conrad Buff (Houghton)

1953 Medal Winner
Secret of the Andes by Ann Nolan Clark (Viking)

Honor Books
Charlotte's Web by E. B. White (Harper)
Moccasin Trail by Eloise Jarvis McGraw (Coward)
Red Sails to Capri by Ann Weil (Viking)
The Bears on Hemlock Mountain by Alice Dalgliesh (Scribner)
Birthdays of Freedom, Vol. 1 by Genevieve Foster (Scribner)

1952 Medal Winner
Ginger Pye by Eleanor Estes (Harcourt)

Honor Books
Americans before Columbus by Elizabeth Baity (Viking)
Minn of the Mississippi by Holling C. Holling (Houghton)
The Defender by Nicholas Kalashnikoff (Scribner)
The Light at Tern Rock by Julia Sauer (Viking)
The Apple and the Arrow by Mary and Conrad Buff (Houghton)

1951 Medal Winner
Amos Fortune, Free Man by Elizabeth Yates (Dutton)

Honor Books
Better Known as Johnny Appleseed by Mabel Leigh Hunt (Lippincott)
Gandhi, Fighter without a Sword by Jeanette Eaton (Morrow)
Abraham Lincoln, Friend of the People by Clara Ingram Judson (Follett)
The Story of Appleby Capple by Anne Parrish (Harper)

1950 Medal Winner
The Door in the Wall by Marguerite de Angeli (Doubleday)

Honor Books

Tree of Freedom by Rebecca Caudill (Viking)

The Blue Cat of Castle Town by Catherine Coblentz (Longmans)

Kildee House by Rutherford Montgomery (Doubleday)

George Washington by Genevieve Foster (Scribner)

Song of the Pines: A Story of Norwegian Lumbering in Wisconsin by Walter and
   Marion Havighurst (Winston)

1949 Medal Winner

King of the Wind by Marguerite Henry (Rand McNally)

Honor Books

Seabird by Holling C. Holling (Houghton)

Daughter of the Mountains by Louise Rankin (Viking)

My Father's Dragon by Ruth S. Gannett (Random House)

Story of the Negro by Arna Bontemps (Knopf)

1948 Medal Winner

The Twenty-One Balloons by William Pène du Bois (Viking)

Honor Books

Pancakes-Paris by Claire Huchet Bishop (Viking)

Li Lun, Lad of Courage by Carolyn Treffinger (Abingdon)

The Quaint and Curious Quest of Johnny Longfoot by Catherine Besterman
   (Bobbs-Merrill)

The Cow-Tail Switch, and Other West African Stories by Harold Courlander
   (Holt)

Misty of Chincoteague by Marguerite Henry (Rand McNally)

1947 Medal Winner

Miss Hickory by Carolyn Sherwin Bailey (Viking)

Honor Books

Wonderful Year by Nancy Barnes (Messner)

Big Tree by Mary and Conrad Buff (Viking)

The Heavenly Tenants by William Maxwell (Harper)

The Avion My Uncle Flew by Cyrus Fisher, pseud. (Darwin L. Teilhet)
   (Appleton)

The Hidden Treasure of Glaston by Eleanor Jewett (Viking)

1946 Medal Winner

Strawberry Girl by Lois Lenski (Lippincott)

Honor Books

Justin Morgan Had a Horse by Marguerite Henry (Rand McNally)

The Moved-Outers by Florence Crannell Means (Houghton)

Bhimsa, the Dancing Bear by Christine Weston (Scribner)

New Found World by Katherine Shippen (Viking)

1945 Medal Winner
Rabbit Hill by Robert Lawson (Viking)

Honor Books
The Hundred Dresses by Eleanor Estes (Harcourt)
The Silver Pencil by Alice Dalgliesh (Scribner)
Abraham Lincoln's World by Genevieve Foster (Scribner)
Lone Journey: The Life of Roger Williams by Jeanette Eaton (Harcourt)

1944 Medal Winner
Johnny Tremain by Esther Forbes (Houghton)

Honor Books
These Happy Golden Years by Laura Ingalls Wilder (Harper)
Fog Magic by Julia Sauer (Viking)
Rufus M. by Eleanor Estes (Harcourt)
Mountain Born by Elizabeth Yates (Coward)

1943 Medal Winner
Adam of the Road by Elizabeth Janet Gray (Viking)

Honor Books
The Middle Moffat by Eleanor Estes (Harcourt)
Have You Seen Tom Thumb? by Mabel Leigh Hunt (Lippincott)

1942 Medal Winner
The Matchlock Gun by Walter Edmonds (Dodd)

Honor Books
Little Town on the Prairie by Laura Ingalls Wilder (Harper)
George Washington's World by Genevieve Foster (Scribner)
Indian Captive: The Story of Mary Jemison by Lois Lenski
    (Lippincott)
Down Ryton Water by Eva Roe Gaggin (Viking)

1941 Medal Winner
Call It Courage by Armstrong Sperry (Macmillan)

Honor Books
Blue Willow by Doris Gates (Viking)
Young Mac of Fort Vancouver by Mary Jane Carr (Crowell)
The Long Winter by Laura Ingalls Wilder (Harper)
Nansen by Anna Gertrude Hall (Viking)

1940 Medal Winner
Daniel Boone by James Daugherty (Viking)

Honor Books
The Singing Tree by Kate Seredy (Viking)
Runner of the Mountain Tops: The Life of Louis Agassiz by Mabel Robinson
    (Random House)
By the Shores of Silver Lake by Laura Ingalls Wilder (Harper)
Boy with a Pack by Stephen W. Meader (Harcourt)

1939 Medal Winner
Thimble Summer by Elizabeth Enright (Rinehart)

Honor Books
Nino by Valenti Angelo (Viking)
Mr. Popper's Penguins by Richard and Florence Atwater (Little, Brown)
Hello the Boat! by Phyllis Crawford (Holt)
Leader by Destiny: George Washington, Man and Patriot by Jeanette Eaton
    (Harcourt)
Penn by Elizabeth Janet Gray (Viking)

1938 Medal Winner
The White Stag by Kate Seredy (Viking)

Honor Books
Pecos Bill: The Greatest Cowboy of All Time by James Cloyd Bowman
    (Little, Brown)
Bright Island by Mabel Robinson (Random House)
On the Banks of Plum Creek by Laura Ingalls Wilder (Harper)

1937 Medal Winner
Roller Skates by Ruth Sawyer (Viking)

Honor Books
Phebe Fairchild: Her Book by Lois Lenski (Stokes)
Whistler's Van by Idwal Jones (Viking)
The Golden Basket by Ludwig Bemelmans (Viking)
Winterbound by Margery Bianco (Viking)
The Codfish Musket by Agnes Hewes (Doubleday)
Audubon by Constance Rourke (Harcourt)

1936 Medal Winner
Caddie Woodlawn by Carol Ryrie Brink (Macmillan)

Honor Books
Honk, the Moose by Phil Stong (Dodd)
The Good Master by Kate Seredy (Viking)
Young Walter Scott by Elizabeth Janet Gray (Viking)
All Sail Set: A Romance of the "Flying Cloud" by Armstrong Sperry (Winston)

1935 Medal Winner
Dobry by Monica Shannon (Viking)

Honor Books
Pageant of Chinese History by Elizabeth Seeger (Longmans)
Davy Crockett by Constance Rourke (Harcourt)
Day on Skates: The Story of a Dutch Picnic by Hilda Von Stockum (Harper)

1934 Medal Winner
Invincible Louisa: The Story of the Author of Little Women by Cornelia Meigs
    (Little, Brown)

Honor Books

The Forgotten Daughter by Caroline Snedeker (Doubleday)
Swords of Steel by Elsie Singmaster (Houghton)
ABC Bunny by Wanda Gág (Coward)
Winged Girl of Knossos by Erik Berry, pseud. (Allena Best) (Appleton)
New Land by Sarah Schmidt (McBride)
Big Tree of Bunlahy: Stories of My Own Countryside by Padraic Colum
    (Macmillan)
Glory of the Seas by Agnes Hewes (Knopf)
Apprentice of Florence by Ann Kyle (Houghton)

1933 Medal Winner

Young Fu of the Upper Yangtze by Elizabeth Lewis (Winston)

Honor Books

Swift Rivers by Cornelia Meigs (Little, Brown)
The Railroad to Freedom: A Story of the Civil War by Hildegarde Swift (Harcourt)
Children of the Soil: A Story of Scandinavia by Nora Burglon (Doubleday)

1932 Medal Winner

Waterless Mountain by Laura Adams Armer (Longmans)

Honor Books

The Fairy Circus by Dorothy P. Lathrop (Macmillan)
Calico Bush by Rachel Field (Macmillan)
Boy of the South Seas by Eunice Tietjens (Coward-McCann)
Out of the Flame by Eloise Lownsbery (Longmans)
Jane's Island by Marjorie Allee (Houghton)
Truce of the Wolf and Other Tales of Old Italy by Mary Gould Davis (Harcourt)

1931 Medal Winner

The Cat Who Went to Heaven by Elizabeth Coatsworth (Macmillan)

Honor Books

Floating Island by Anne Parrish (Harper)
The Dark Star of Itza: The Story of a Pagan Princess by Alida Malkus (Harcourt)
Queer Person by Ralph Hubbard (Doubleday)
Mountains Are Free by Julie Davis Adams (Dutton)
Spice and the Devil's Cave by Agnes Hewes (Knopf)
Meggy MacIntosh by Elizabeth Janet Gray (Doubleday)
Garram the Hunter: A Boy of the Hill Tribes by Herbert Best (Doubleday)
Ood-Le-Uk the Wanderer by Alice Lide and Margaret Johansen (Little, Brown)

1930 Medal Winner

Hitty, Her First Hundred Years by Rachel Field (Macmillan)

Honor Books

A Daughter of the Seine: The Life of Madame Roland by Jeanette Eaton (Harper)
Pran of Albania by Elizabeth Miller (Doubleday)

Jumping-Off Place by Marion Hurd McNeely (Longmans)
The Tangle-Coated Horse and Other Tales by Ella Young (Longmans)
Vaino by Julia Davis Adams (Dutton)
Little Blacknose by Hildegarde Swift (Harcourt)

1929 Medal Winner
The Trumpeter of Krakow by Eric P. Kelly (Macmillan)

Honor Books
The Pigtail of Ah Lee Ben Loo by John Bennett (Longmans)
Millions of Cats by Wanda Gág (Coward)
The Boy Who Was by Grace Hallock (Dutton)
Clearing Weather by Cornelia Meigs (Little, Brown)
Runaway Papoose by Grace Moon (Doubleday)
Tod of the Fens by Elinor Whitney (Macmillan)

1928 Medal Winner
Gay Neck, the Story of a Pigeon by Dhan Gopal Mukerji (Dutton)

Honor Books
The Wonder Smith and His Son by Ella Young (Longmans)
Downright Dencey by Caroline Snedeker (Doubleday)

1927 Medal Winner
Smoky, the Cowhorse by Will James (Scribner)

Honor Books
[None recorded]

1926 Medal Winner
Shen of the Sea by Arthur Bowie Chrisman (Dutton)

Honor Book
The Voyagers: Being Legends and Romances of Atlantic Discovery by Padraic
    Colum (Macmillan)

1925 Medal Winner
Tales from Silver Lands by Charles Finger (Doubleday)

Honor Books
Nicholas: A Manhattan Christmas Story by Annie Carroll Moore (Putnam)
The Dream Coach by Anne Parrish (Macmillan)

1924 Medal Winner
The Dark Frigate by Charles Hawes (Little, Brown)

Honor Books
[None recorded]

1923 Medal Winner
The Voyages of Doctor Dolittle by Hugh Lofting (Stokes)

Honor Books
[None recorded]

1922 Medal Winner
The Story of Mankind by Hendrik Willem van Loon (Liveright)

Honor Books
The Great Quest by Charles Hawes (Little, Brown)
Cedric the Forester by Bernard Marshall (Appleton)
The Old Tobacco Shop: A True Account of What Befell a Little Boy in Search of Adventure by William Bowen (Macmillan)
The Golden Fleece and the Heroes Who Lived Before Achilles by Padraic Colum (Macmillan)
The Windy Hill by Cornelia Meigs (Macmillan)

Caldecott Medal Winners and Honor Books, 1938–2008

2008 Medal Winner
The Invention of Hugo Cabret by Brian Selznick (Scholastic Press, an imprint of Scholastic)

Honor Books
Henry's Freedom Box: A True Story from the Underground Railroad illustrated by Kadir Nelson, written by Ellen Levine (Scholastic Press, an imprint of Scholastic)
First the Egg written and illustrated by Laura Vaccaro Seeger (Roaring Brook/Neal Porter)
The Wall: Growing up behind the Iron Curtain written and illustrated by Peter Sís (Farrar/Frances Foster)
Knuffle Bunny Too: A Case of Mistaken Identity written and illustrated by Mo Willems (Hyperion)

2007 Medal Winner
Flotsam by David Wiesner (Clarion)

Honor Books
Gone Wild: An Endangered Animal Alphabet by David McLimans (Walker)
Moses: When Harriet Tubman Led Her People to Freedom illustrated by Kadir Nelson, written by Carole Boston Weatherford (Hyperion/Jump at the Sun)

2006 Medal Winner
The Hello, Goodbye Window illustrated by Chris Raschka and written by Norton Juster (Michael di Capua Books/Hyperion Books for Children)

Honor Books
Rosa illustrated by Bryan Collier and written by Nikki Giovanni (Henry Holt and Company)

Zen Shorts illustrated and written by Jon J. Muth (Scholastic Press)
Hot Air: The (Mostly) True Story of the First Hot-Air Balloon Ride illustrated and written by Marjorie Priceman (An Anne Schwartz Book/Atheneum Books for Young Readers/Simon & Schuster)
Song of the Water Boatman and Other Pond Poems illustrated by Beckie Prange and written by Joyce Sidman (Houghton Mifflin Company)

2005 Medal Winner
Kitten's First Full Moon by Kevin Henkes (Greenwillow Books/HarperCollins Publishers)

Honor Books
The Red Book by Barbara Lehman (Houghton Mifflin Company)
Coming on Home Soon illustrated by E. B. Lewis and written by Jacqueline Woodson (G. P. Putnam's Son's/Penguin Young Readers Group)
Knuffle Bunny: A Cautionary Tale illustrated and written by Mo Willems (Hyperion Books for Children)

2004 Medal Winner
The Man Who Walked between the Towers by Mordicai Gerstein (Roaring Brook Press/Millbrook Press)

Honor Books
Ella Sarah Gets Dressed by Margaret Chodos-Irvine (Harcourt)
What Do You Do with a Tail Like This? illustrated and written by Steve Jenkins and Robin Page (Houghton Mifflin Company)
Don't Let the Pigeon Drive the Bus! by Mo Willems (Hyperion)

2003 Medal Winner
My Friend Rabbit by Eric Rohmann (Roaring Brook Press/Millbrook Press)

Honor Books
The Spider and the Fly illustrated by Tony DiTerlizzi and written by Mary Howitt (Simon & Schuster Books for Young Readers)
Hondo and Fabian by Peter McCarty (Henry Holt & Co.)
Noah's Ark by Jerry Pinkney (SeaStar Books, a division of North-South Books Inc.)

2002 Medal Winner
The Three Pigs by David Wiesner (Clarion/Houghton Mifflin)

Honor Books
The Dinosaurs of Waterhouse Hawkins illustrated by Brian Selznick and written by Barbara Kerley (Scholastic)
Martin's Big Words: The Life of Dr. Martin Luther King, Jr. illustrated by Bryan Collier and written by Doreen Rappaport (Jump at the Sun/Hyperion)
The Stray Dog by Marc Simont (HarperCollins)

2001 Medal Winner
So You Want to Be President? illustrated by David Small and written by Judith St. George (Philomel)

Honor Books

Casey at the Bat: A Ballad of the Republic Sung in the Year 1888 illustrated by
    Christopher Bing and written by Ernest Lawrence Thayer (Handprint)
Click, Clack, Moo: Cows That Type illustrated by Betsy Lewin and written by
    Doreen Cronin (Simon & Schuster)
Olivia by Ian Falconer (Atheneum)

2000 Medal Winner

Joseph Had a Little Overcoat by Simms Taback (Viking)

Honor Books

A Child's Calendar illustrated by Trina Schart Hyman and text by John
    Updike (Holiday House)
Sector 7 by David Wiesner (Clarion Books)
When Sophie Gets Angry—Really, Really Angry . . . by Molly Bang (Scholastic)
The Ugly Duckling illustrated by Jerry Pinkney and text by Hans Christian
    Andersen, adapted by Jerry Pinkney (Morrow)

1999 Medal Winner

Snowflake Bentley illustrated by Mary Azarian and text by Jacqueline Briggs
    Martin (Houghton Mifflin)

Honor Books

Duke Ellington: The Piano Prince and His Orchestra illustrated by Brian
    Pinkney and text by Andrea Davis Pinkney (Hyperion)
No, David! by David Shannon (Blue Sky/Scholastic)
Snow by Uri Shulevitz (Farrar)
Tibet: Through the Red Box by Peter Sís (Frances Foster)

1998 Medal Winner

Rapunzel by Paul O. Zelinsky (Dutton)

Honor Books

The Gardener illustrated by David Small and text by Sarah Stewart (Farrar)
Harlem illustrated by Christopher Myers and text by Walter Dean Myers
    (Scholastic)
There Was an Old Lady Who Swallowed a Fly by Simms Taback (Viking)

1997 Medal Winner

Golem by David Wisniewski (Clarion)

Honor Books

Hush! A Thai Lullaby illustrated by Holly Meade and text by Minfong Ho
    (Melanie Kroupa/Orchard Books)
The Graphic Alphabet by David Pelletier (Orchard Books)
The Paperboy by Dav Pilkey (Richard Jackson/Orchard Books)
Starry Messenger by Peter Sís (Frances Foster Books/Farrar, Straus, and
    Giroux)

1996 Medal Winner
Officer Buckle and Gloria by Peggy Rathmann (G. P. Putnam's Sons)

Honor Books
Alphabet City by Stephen T. Johnson (Viking)
Zin! Zin! Zin! a Violin illustrated by Marjorie Priceman and text by Lloyd Moss (Simon & Schuster)
The Faithful Friend illustrated by Brian Pinkney and text by Robert D. San Souci (Simon & Schuster)
Tops and Bottoms adapted and illustrated by Janet Stevens (Harcourt)

1995 Medal Winner
Smoky Night illustrated by David Diaz and text by Eve Bunting (Harcourt Brace)

Honor Books
John Henry illustrated by Jerry Pinkney and text by Julius Lester (Dial)
Swamp Angel illustrated by Paul O. Zelinsky and text by Anne Isaacs (Dutton)
Time Flies by Eric Rohmann (Crown)

1994 Medal Winner
Grandfather's Journey by Allen Say; text edited by Walter Lorraine (Houghton)

Honor Books
Peppe the Lamplighter illustrated by Ted Lewin and text by Elisa Bartone (Lothrop)
In the Small, Small Pond by Denise Fleming (Holt)
Raven: A Trickster Tale from the Pacific Northwest by Gerald McDermott (Harcourt)
Owen by Kevin Henkes (Greenwillow)
Yo! Yes? illustrated by Chris Raschka; text edited by Richard Jackson (Orchard)

1993 Medal Winner
Mirette on the High Wire by Emily Arnold McCully (Putnam)

Honor Books
The Stinky Cheese Man and Other Fairly Stupid Tales illustrated by Lane Smith and text by Jon Scieszka (Viking)
Seven Blind Mice by Ed Young (Philomel Books)
Working Cotton illustrated by Carole Byard and text by Sherley Anne Williams (Harcourt)

1992 Medal Winner
Tuesday by David Wiesner (Clarion Books)

Honor Book
Tar Beach by Faith Ringgold (Crown Publishers, Inc., a Random House Co.)

1991 Medal Winner
Black and White by David Macaulay (Houghton)

Honor Books

Puss in Boots illustrated by Fred Marcellino and text by Charles Perrault, translated by Malcolm Arthur (Di Capua/Farrar)

"More More More," Said the Baby: Three Love Stories by Vera B. Williams (Greenwillow)

1990 Medal Winner

Lon Po Po: A Red Riding Hood Story from China by Ed Young (Philomel)

Honor Books

Bill Peet: An Autobiography by Bill Peet (Houghton)

Color Zoo by Lois Ehlert (Lippincott)

The Talking Eggs: A Folktale from the American South illustrated by Jerry Pinkney and text by Robert D. San Souci (Dial)

Hershel and the Hanukkah Goblins illustrated by Trina Schart Hyman and text by Eric Kimmel (Holiday House)

1989 Medal Winner

Song and Dance Man illustrated by Stephen Gammell and text by Karen Ackerman (Knopf)

Honor Books

The Boy of the Three-Year Nap illustrated by Allen Say and text by Dianne Snyder (Houghton)

Free Fall by David Wiesner (Lothrop)

Goldilocks and the Three Bears by James Marshall (Dial)

Mirandy and Brother Wind illustrated by Jerry Pinkney and text by Patricia C. McKissack (Knopf)

1988 Medal Winner

Owl Moon illustrated by John Schoenherr and text by Jane Yolen (Philomel)

Honor Book

Mufaro's Beautiful Daughters: An African Tale by John Steptoe (Lothrop)

1987 Medal Winner

Hey, Al illustrated by Richard Egielski and text by Arthur Yorinks (Farrar)

Honor Books

The Village of Round and Square Houses by Ann Grifalconi (Little, Brown)

Alphabatics by Suse MacDonald (Bradbury)

Rumpelstiltskin by Paul O. Zelinsky (Dutton)

1986 Medal Winner

The Polar Express by Chris Van Allsburg (Houghton)

Honor Books

The Relatives Came illustrated by Stephen Gammell and text by Cynthia Rylant (Bradbury)

King Bidgood's in the Bathtub illustrated by Don Wood and text by Audrey Wood (Harcourt)

1985 Medal Winner

Saint George and the Dragon illustrated by Trina Schart Hyman and text
retold by Margaret Hodges (Little, Brown)

Honor Books

Hansel and Gretel illustrated by Paul O. Zelinsky and text retold by Rika
Lesser (Dodd)

Have You Seen My Duckling? by Nancy Tafuri (Greenwillow)

The Story of Jumping Mouse: A Native American Legend retold and illustrated
by John Steptoe (Lothrop)

1984 Medal Winner

The Glorious Flight: Across the Channel with Louis Bleriot by Alice and Martin
Provensen (Viking)

Honor Books

Little Red Riding Hood retold and illustrated by Trina Schart Hyman
(Holiday)

Ten, Nine, Eight by Molly Bang (Greenwillow)

1983 Medal Winner

Shadow translated and illustrated by Marcia Brown; original text in French
by Blaise Cendrars (Scribner)

Honor Books

A Chair for My Mother by Vera B. Williams (Greenwillow)

When I Was Young in the Mountains illustrated by Diane Goode and text by
Cynthia Rylant (Dutton)

1982 Medal Winner

Jumanji by Chris Van Allsburg (Houghton)

Honor Books

Where the Buffaloes Begin illustrated by Stephen Gammell and text by Olaf
Baker (Warne)

On Market Street illustrated by Anita Lobel and text by Arnold Lobel
(Greenwillow)

Outside over There by Maurice Sendak (Harper)

A Visit to William Blake's Inn: Poems for Innocent and Experienced Travelers
illustrated by Alice and Martin Provensen and text by Nancy Willard
(Harcourt)

1981 Medal Winner

Fables by Arnold Lobel (Harper)

Honor Books

The Bremen-Town Musicians retold and illustrated by Ilse Plume (Doubleday)

The Grey Lady and the Strawberry Snatcher by Molly Bang (Four Winds)

Mice Twice by Joseph Low (McElderry/Atheneum)

Truck by Donald Crews (Greenwillow)

1980 Medal Winner

Ox-Cart Man illustrated by Barbara Cooney and text by Donald Hall (Viking)

Honor Books

Ben's Trumpet by Rachel Isadora (Greenwillow)
The Garden of Abdul Gasazi by Chris Van Allsburg (Houghton)
The Treasure by Uri Shulevitz (Farrar)

1979 Medal Winner

The Girl Who Loved Wild Horses by Paul Goble (Bradbury)

Honor Books

Freight Train by Donald Crews (Greenwillow)
The Way to Start a Day illustrated by Peter Parnall and text by Byrd Baylor (Scribner)

1978 Medal Winner

Noah's Ark by Peter Spier (Doubleday)

Honor Books

Castle by David Macaulay (Houghton)
It Could Always Be Worse retold and illustrated by Margot Zemach (Farrar)

1977 Medal Winner

Ashanti to Zulu: African Traditions illustrated by Leo and Diane Dillon and text by Margaret Musgrove (Dial)

Honor Books

The Amazing Bone by William Steig (Farrar)
The Contest retold and illustrated by Nonny Hogrogian (Greenwillow)
Fish for Supper by M. B. Goffstein (Dial)
Golem: A Jewish Legend by Beverly Brodsky McDermott (Lippincott)
Hawk, I'm Your Brother illustrated by Peter Parnall and text by Byrd Baylor (Scribner)

1976 Medal Winner

Why Mosquitoes Buzz in People's Ears: A West African Tale illustrated by Leo and Diane Dillon and text retold by Verna Aardema (Dial)

Honor Books

The Desert Is Theirs illustrated by Peter Parnall and text by Byrd Baylor (Scribner)
Strega Nona by Tomie de Paola (Prentice-Hall)

1975 Medal Winner

Arrow to the Sun by Gerald McDermott (Viking)

Honor Books

Jambo Means Hello: Swahili Alphabet Book illustrated by Tom Feelings and text by Muriel Feelings (Dial)

1974 Medal Winner

Duffy and the Devil illustrated by Margot Zemach and retold by Harve
	Zemach (Farrar)

Honor Books

Three Jovial Huntsmen: A Mother Goose Rhyme by Susan Jeffers (Bradbury)
Cathedral by David Macaulay (Houghton)

1973 Medal Winner

The Funny Little Woman illustrated by Blair Lent and text retold by Arlene
	Mosel (Dutton)

Honor Books

Anansi the Spider: A Tale from the Ashanti adapted and illustrated by Gerald
	McDermott (Holt)
Hosie's Alphabet illustrated by Leonard Baskin and text by Hosea Tobias and
	Lisa Baskin (Viking)
Snow-White and the Seven Dwarfs illustrated by Nancy Ekholm Burkert and
	text translated by Randall Jarrell, retold from the Brothers Grimm
	(Farrar)
When Clay Sings illustrated by Tom Bahti and text by Byrd Baylor (Scribner)

1972 Medal Winner

One Fine Day retold and illustrated by Nonny Hogrogian (Macmillan)

Honor Books

Hildilid's Night illustrated by Arnold Lobel and text by Cheli Durán Ryan
	(Macmillan)
If All the Seas Were One Sea by Janina Domanska (Macmillan)
Moja Means One: Swahili Counting Book illustrated by Tom Feelings and text
	by Muriel Feelings (Dial)

1971 Medal Winner

A Story, a Story retold and illustrated by Gail E. Haley (Atheneum)

Honor Books

The Angry Moon illustrated by Blair Lent and text retold by William Sleator
	(Atlantic)
Frog and Toad Are Friends by Arnold Lobel (Harper)
In the Night Kitchen by Maurice Sendak (Harper)

1970 Medal Winner

Sylvester and the Magic Pebble by William Steig (Windmill Books)

Honor Books

Goggles! by Ezra Jack Keats (Macmillan)
Alexander and the Wind-Up Mouse by Leo Lionni (Pantheon)
Pop Corn and Ma Goodness illustrated by Robert Andrew Parker and text by
	Edna Mitchell Preston (Viking)
Thy Friend, Obadiah by Brinton Turkle (Viking)

The Judge: An Untrue Tale illustrated by Margot Zemach and text by Harve Zemach (Farrar)

1969 Medal Winner
The Fool of the World and the Flying Ship illustrated by Uri Shulevitz and text retold by Arthur Ransome (Farrar)

Honor Books
Why the Sun and the Moon Live in the Sky illustrated by Blair Lent and text by Elphinstone Dayrell (Houghton)

1968 Medal Winner
Drummer Hoff illustrated by Ed Emberley and text adapted by Barbara Emberley (Prentice-Hall)

Honor Books
Frederick by Leo Lionni (Pantheon)
Seashore Story by Taro Yashima (Viking)
The Emperor and the Kite illustrated by Ed Young and text by Jane Yolen (World)

1967 Medal Winner
Sam, Bangs and Moonshine by Evaline Ness (Holt)

Honor Book
One Wide River to Cross illustrated by Ed Emberley and text adapted by Barbara Emberley (Prentice-Hall)

1966 Medal Winner
Always Room for One More illustrated by Nonny Hogrogian and text by Sorche Nic Leodhas, pseudo. (Leclair Alger) (Holt)

Honor Books
Hide and Seek Fog illustrated by Roger Duvoisin and text by Alvin Tresselt (Lothrop)
Just Me by Marie Hall Ets (Viking)
Tom Tit Tot retold and illustrated by Evaline Ness (Scribner)

1965 Medal Winner
May I Bring a Friend? illustrated by Beni Montresor and text by Beatrice Schenk de Regniers (Atheneum)

Honor Books
Rain Makes Applesauce illustrated by Marvin Bileck and text by Julian Scheer (Holiday)
The Wave illustrated by Blair Lent and text by Margaret Hodges (Houghton)
A Pocketful of Cricket illustrated by Evaline Ness and text by Rebecca Caudill (Holt)

1964 Medal Winner
Where the Wild Things Are by Maurice Sendak (Harper)

Honor Books

Swimmy by Leo Lionni (Pantheon)

All in the Morning Early illustrated by Evaline Ness and text by Sorche Nic Leodhas, pseud. (Leclaire Alger) (Holt)

Mother Goose and Nursery Rhymes illustrated by Philip Reed (Atheneum)

1963 Medal Winner

The Snowy Day by Ezra Jack Keats (Viking)

Honor Books

The Sun Is a Golden Earring illustrated by Bernarda Bryson and text by Natalia M. Belting (Holt)

Mr. Rabbit and the Lovely Present illustrated by Maurice Sendak and text by Charlotte Zolotow (Harper)

1962 Medal Winner

Once a Mouse retold and illustrated by Marcia Brown (Scribner)

Honor Books

Fox Went out on a Chilly Night: An Old Song by Peter Spier (Doubleday)

Little Bear's Visit illustrated by Maurice Sendak and text by Else H. Minarik (Harper)

The Day We Saw the Sun Come up illustrated by Adrienne Adams and text by Alice E. Goudey (Scribner)

1961 Medal Winner

Baboushka and the Three Kings illustrated by Nicolas Sidjakov and text by Ruth Robbins (Parnassus)

Honor Book

Inch by Inch by Leo Lionni (Obolensky)

1960 Medal Winner

Nine Days to Christmas illustrated by Marie Hall Ets and text by Marie Hall Ets and Aurora Labastida (Viking)

Honor Books

Houses from the Sea illustrated by Adrienne Adams and text by Alice E. Goudey (Scribner)

The Moon Jumpers illustrated by Maurice Sendak and text by Janice May Udry (Harper)

1959 Medal Winner

Chanticleer and the Fox illustrated by Barbara Cooney and text adapted from Chaucer's Canterbury Tales by Barbara Cooney (Crowell)

Honor Books

The House That Jack Built: La Maison Que Jacques A Batie by Antonio Frasconi (Harcourt)

What Do You Say, Dear? illustrated by Maurice Sendak and text by Sesyle Joslin (W. R. Scott)

Umbrella by Taro Yashima (Viking)

1958 Medal Winner
Time of Wonder by Robert McCloskey (Viking)

Honor Books
Fly High Fly Low by Don Freeman (Viking)
Anatole and the Cat illustrated by Paul Galdone and text by Eve Titus
    (McGraw-Hill)

1957 Medal Winner
A Tree Is Nice illustrated by Marc Simont and text by Janice May Udry
    (Harper)

Honor Books
Mr. Penny's Race Horse by Marie Hall Ets (Viking)
1 is One by Tasha Tudor (Walck)
Anatole illustrated by Paul Galdone and text by Eve Titus (McGraw-Hill)
Gillespie and the Guards illustrated by James Daugherty and text by
    Benjamin Elkin (Viking)
Lion by William Pène du Bois (Viking)

1956 Medal Winner
Frog Went A-Courtin' illustrated by Feodor Rojankovsky and text retold by
    John Langstaff (Harcourt)

Honor Books
Play with Me by Marie Hall Ets (Viking)
Crow Boy by Taro Yashima (Viking)

1955 Medal Winner
Cinderella, or the Little Glass Slipper illustrated by Marcia Brown and text
    translated from Charles Perrault by Marcia Brown (Scribner)

Honor Books
Book of Nursery and Mother Goose Rhymes illustrated by Marguerite de
    Angeli (Doubleday)
Wheel on the Chimney illustrated by Tibor Gergely and text by Margaret
    Wise Brown (Lippincott)
The Thanksgiving Story illustrated by Helen Sewell and text by Alice
    Dalgliesh (Scribner)

1954 Medal Winner
Madeline's Rescue by Ludwig Bemelmans (Viking)

Honor Books
Journey Cake, Ho! illustrated by Robert McCloskey and text by Ruth Sawyer
    (Viking)
When Will the World Be Mine? The Story of a Snowshoe Rabbit illustrated by
    Jean Charlot and text by Miriam Schlein (W. R. Scott)

The Steadfast Tin Soldier illustrated by Marcia Brown and text by Hans
   Christian Andersen, translated by M. R. James (Scribner)
A Very Special House illustrated by Maurice Sendak and text by Ruth Krauss
   (Harper)
Green Eyes by A. Birnbaum (Capitol)

1953 Medal Winner
The Biggest Bear by Lynd Ward (Houghton)

Honor Books
Puss in Boots illustrated by Marcia Brown and text translated from Charles
   Perrault by Marcia Brown (Scribner)
One Morning in Maine by Robert McCloskey (Viking)
Ape in a Cape: An Alphabet of Odd Animals by Fritz Eichenberg (Harcourt)
The Storm Book illustrated by Margaret Bloy Graham and text by Charlotte
   Zolotow (Harper)
Five Little Monkeys by Juliet Kepes (Houghton)

1952 Medal Winner
Finders Keepers illustrated by Nicolas, pseud. (Nicholas Mordvinoff) and
   text by Will, pseud. (William Lipkind) (Harcourt)

Honor Books
Mr. T. W. Anthony Woo by Marie Hall Ets (Viking)
Skipper John's Cook by Marcia Brown (Scribner)
All Falling Down illustrated by Margaret Bloy Graham and text by Gene
   Zion (Harper)
Bear Party by William Pène du Bois (Viking)
Feather Mountain by Elizabeth Olds (Houghton)

1951 Medal Winner
The Egg Tree by Katherine Milhous (Scribner)

Honor Books
Dick Whittington and His Cat by Marcia Brown (Scribner)
The Two Reds illustrated by Nicolas, pseud. (Nicholas Mordvinoff) and text
   by Will, pseud. (William Lipkind) (Harcourt)
If I Ran the Zoo by Dr. Seuss, pseud. (Theodor Seuss Geisel) (Random
   House)
The Most Wonderful Doll in the World illustrated by Helen Stone and text by
   Phyllis McGinley (Lippincott)
T-Bone, the Baby Sitter by Clare Turlay Newberry (Harper)

1950 Medal Winner
Song of the Swallows by Leo Politi (Scribner)

Honor Books
America's Ethan Allen illustrated by Lynd Ward and text by Stewart
   Holbrook (Houghton)

The Wild Birthday Cake illustrated by Hildegard Woodward and text by
Lavinia R. Davis (Doubleday)

The Happy Day illustrated by Marc Simont and text by Ruth Krauss (Harper)

Bartholomew and the Oobleck by Dr. Seuss, pseud. (Theodor Seuss Geisel)
(Random House)

Henry Fisherman, a Story of the Virgin Islands by Marcia Brown (Scribner's
Sons)

1949 Medal Winner

The Big Snow by Berta and Elmer Hader (Macmillan)

Honor Books

Blueberries for Sal by Robert McCloskey (Viking)

All Around the Town illustrated by Helen Stone and text by Phyllis McGinley
(Lippincott)

Juanita by Leo Politi (Scribner)

Fish in the Air by Kurt Wiese (Viking)

1948 Medal Winner

White Snow Bright Snow illustrated by Roger Duvoisin and text by Alvin
Tresselt (Lothrop)

Honor Books

Stone Soup by Marcia Brown (Scribner)

McElligot's Pool by Dr. Seuss, pseud. (Theodor Seuss Geisel) (Random House)

Bambino the Clown by Georges Schreiber (Viking)

Roger and the Fox illustrated by Hildegard Woodward and text by Lavinia
R. Davis (Doubleday)

Song of Robin Hood illustrated by Virginia Lee Burton and text edited by
Anne Malcolmson (Houghton)

1947 Medal Winner

The Little Island illustrated by Leonard Weisgard and text by Golden
MacDonald, pseud. (Margaret Wise Brown) (Doubleday)

Honor Books

Rain Drop Splash illustrated by Leonard Weisgard and text by Alvin Tresselt
(Lothrop)

Boats on the River illustrated by Jay Hyde Barnum and text by Marjorie
Flack (Viking)

Timothy Turtle illustrated by Tony Palazzo and text by Al Graham (Welch)

Pedro, the Angel of Olvera Street by Leo Politi (Scribner)

Sing in Praise: A Collection of the Best Loved Hymns illustrated by Marjorie
Torrey and text selected by Opal Wheeler (Dutton)

1946 Medal Winner

The Rooster Crows: A Book of American Rhymes and Jingles by Maud and
Miska Petersham (Macmillan)

Honor Books
Little Lost Lamb illustrated by Leonard Weisgard and text by Golden
    MacDonald, pseud. (Margaret Wise Brown) (Doubleday)
Sing Mother Goose illustrated by Marjorie Torrey and music by Opal
    Wheeler (Dutton)
My Mother Is the Most Beautiful Woman in the World illustrated by Ruth
    Gannett and text by Becky Reyher (Lothrop)
You Can Write Chinese by Kurt Wiese (Viking)

1945 Medal Winner
Prayer for a Child illustrated by Elizabeth Orton Jones and text by Rachel
    Field (Macmillan)

Honor Books
Mother Goose illustrated by Tasha Tudor (Oxford University Press)
In the Forest by Marie Hall Ets (Viking)
Yonie Wondernose by Marguerite de Angeli (Doubleday)
The Christmas Anna Angel illustrated by Kate Seredy and text by Ruth
    Sawyer (Viking)

1944 Medal Winner
Many Moons illustrated by Louis Slobodkin and text by James Thurber
    (Harcourt)

Honor Books
Small Rain: Verses from the Bible illustrated by Elizabeth Orton Jones and
    text selected by Jessie Orton Jones (Viking)
Pierre Pidgeon illustrated by Arnold E. Bare and text by Lee Kingman
    (Houghton)
The Mighty Hunter by Berta and Elmer Hader (Macmillan)
A Child's Good Night Book illustrated by Jean Charlot and text by Margaret
    Wise Brown (W. R. Scott)
Good-Luck Horse illustrated by Plato Chan and text by Chih-Yi Chan
    (Whittlesey)

1943 Medal Winner
The Little House by Virginia Lee Burton (Houghton)

Honor Books
Dash and Dart by Mary and Conrad Buff (Viking)
Marshmallow by Clare Turlay Newberry (Harper)

1942 Medal Winner
Make Way for Ducklings by Robert McCloskey (Viking)

Honor Books
An American ABC by Maud and Miska Petersham (Macmillan)
In My Mother's House illustrated by Velino Herrera and text by Ann Nolan
    Clark (Viking)

Paddle-to-the-Sea by Holling C. Holling (Houghton)
Nothing at All by Wanda Gág (Coward)

1941 Medal Winner
They Were Strong and Good by Robert Lawson (Viking)

Honor Book
April's Kittens by Clare Turlay Newberry (Harper)

1940 Medal Winner
Abraham Lincoln by Ingri and Edgar Parin d'Aulaire (Doubleday)

Honor Books
Cock-a-Doodle Doo by Berta and Elmer Hader (Macmillan)
Madeline by Ludwig Bemelmans (Viking)
The Ageless Story by Lauren Ford (Dodd)

1939 Medal Winner
Mei Li by Thomas Handforth (Doubleday)

Honor Books
Andy and the Lion by James Daugherty (Viking)
Barkis by Clare Turlay Newberry (Harper)
The Forest Pool by Laura Adams Armer (Longmans)
Snow White and the Seven Dwarfs by Wanda Gág (Coward)
Wee Gillis illustrated by Robert Lawson and text by Munro Leaf (Viking)

1938 Medal Winner
Animals of the Bible, A Picture Book illustrated by Dorothy P. Lathrop and
text selected by Helen Dean Fish (Lippincott)

Honor Books
Four and Twenty Blackbirds illustrated by Robert Lawson and text compiled
by Helen Dean Fish (Stokes)
Seven Simeons: A Russian Tale retold and illustrated by Boris Artzybasheff
(Viking)

Coretta Scott King Book Award, 1970–2008

2008 Winners
Author Award Winner
Elijah of Buxton by Christopher Paul Curtis (published by Scholastic)
Author Honor Books
November Blues by Sharon M. Draper (published by Atheneum Books for
Young Adults)
Twelve Rounds to Glory: The Story of Muhammad Ali by Charles R. Smith Jr.
and illustrated by Bryan Collier (published by Candlewick Press)

Illustrator Award Winner

Let It Shine: Three Favorite Spirituals by Ashley Bryan (published by Atheneum Books for Young Readers)

Illustrator Honor Books

The Secret Olivia Told Me by Nancy Devard and written by N. Joy (published by Just Us Books)

Jazz on a Saturday Night by Leo and Diane Dillon (published by Scholastic Blue Sky Press)

2007 Winners

Author Award Winner

Copper Sun by Sharon Draper (published by Simon & Schuster/Atheneum Books for Young Readers)

Author Honor Books

The Road to Paris by Nikki Grimes (published by G. P. Putnum's Sons, a division of Penguin Young Readers Group)

Illustrator Award Winner

Moses: When Harriet Tubman Led Her People to Freedom illustrated by Kadir Nelson, written by Carole Boston Weatherford (published by Jump at the Sun/Hyperion Books for Children)

Illustrator Honor Books

Jazz illustrated by Christopher Myers and written by Walter Dean Myers (published by Holiday House)

Poetry for Young People: Langston Hughes illustrated by Benny Andrews and edited by David Roessel and Arnold Rampersad (published by Sterling)

2006 Winners

Author Award Winner

Day of Tears: A Novel in Dialogue by Julius Lester (published by Jump at the Sun, an imprint of Hyperion Books for Children)

Author Honor Books

Maritcha: A Nineteenth-Century American Girl by Tonya Bolden (published by Harry N. Abrams)

Dark Sons by Nikki Grimes (published by Jump at the Sun, an imprint of Hyperion Books for Children)

A Wreath for Emmett Till by Marilyn Nelson and illustrated by Philippe Lardy (published by Houghton Mifflin Company)

Illustrator Award Winner

Rosa by Nikki Giovanni and illustrated by Bryan Collier (published by Henry Holt and Company)

Illustrator Honor Books

Brothers in Hope: The Story of the Lost Boys of Sudan by Mary Williams and illustrated by R. Gregory Christie (published by Lee and Low Books)

2005 Winners

Author Award Winner

Remember: The Journey to School Integration by Toni Morrison (Houghton Mifflin)

Author Honor Books

The Legend of Buddy Bush by Shelia P. Moses (Margaret K. McElderry Books, an imprint of Simon & Schuster)

Who Am I without Him? Short Stories about Girls and the Boys in Their Lives by Sharon G. Flake (Jump at the Sun/Hyperion Books for Children)

Fortune's Bones: The Manumission Requiem by Marilyn Nelson (Front Street)

Illustrator Award Book

Ellington Was Not a Street illustrated by Kadir A. Nelson and text by Ntozake Shange (Simon & Schuster Books for Young Readers)

Illustrator Honor Books

God Bless the Child illustrated by Jerry Pinkney and text by Billie Holiday and Arthur Herzog Jr. (Amistad, an imprint of HarperCollins Publishers)

The People Could Fly: The Picture Book illustrated by Leo and Diane Dillon and text by Virginia Hamilton (Alfred A. Knopf, an imprint of Random House Children's)

2004 Winners

Author Award Winner

The First Part Last by Angela Johnson (Simon & Schuster Books for Young Readers)

Author Honor Books

Days of Jubilee: The End of Slavery in the United States by Patricia C. and Fredrick L. McKissack (Scholastic)

Locomotion by Jacqueline Woodson (Grosset & Dunlap)

The Battle of Jericho by Sharon Draper (Atheneum Books for Young Readers)

Illustrator Award Book

Beautiful Blackbird by Ashley Bryan (Atheneum Books for Young Readers)

Illustrator Honor Books

Almost to Freedom illustrated by Colin Bootman and text by Vaunda Micheaux Nelson (Carolrhoda Books)

Thunder Rose illustrated by Kadir Nelson and text by Jerdine Nolen (Silver Whistle)

2003 Winners

Author Award Winner

Bronx Masquerade by Nikki Grimes (Dial Books for Young Readers)

Author Honor Books

The Red Rose Box by Brenda Woods (G. P. Putnam's Sons)

Talkin' about Bessie: The Story of Aviator Elizabeth Coleman by Nikki Grimes (Orchard Books/Scholastic)

Illustrator Award Winner

Talkin' about Bessie: The Story of Aviator Elizabeth Coleman illustrated by E. B. Lewis and text by Nikki Grimes (Orchard Books/Scholastic)

Illustrator Honor Books

Rap a Tap Tap: Here's Bojangles—Think of That! illustrated and text by Leo and Diane Dillion (Blue Sky Press/Scholastic)

Visiting Langston illustrated by Bryan Collier and text by Willie Perdomo (Henry Holt & Co.)

2002 Winners

Author Award Winner

The Land by Mildred D. Taylor (Phyllis Fogelman Books/Penguin Putnam)

Author Honor Books

Money Hungry by Sharon G. Flake (Jump at the Sun/Hyperion)
Carver: A Life in Poems by Marilyn Nelson (Front Street)

Illustrator Award Winner

Goin' Someplace Special illustrated by Jerry Pinkney and text by Patricia McKissack (Anne Schwartz Book/Atheneum)

Illustrator Honor Books

Martin's Big Words illustrated by Bryan Collier and text by Doreen Rappaport (Jump at the Sun/Hyperion)

2001 Winners

Author Award Winner

Miracle's Boys by Jacqueline Woodson (G. P. Putnam's Sons)

Author Honor Books

Let It Shine: Stories of Black Women Freedom Fighters by Andrea Davis Pinkney and illustrated by Stephen Alcorn (Gulliver Books, Harcourt)

Illustrator Award Winner

Uptown by Bryan Collier (Henry Holt)

Illustrator Honor Books

Freedom River illustrated by Bryan Collier and text by Doreen Rappaport (Jump at the Sun/Hyperion)

Only Passing Through: The Story of Sojourner Truth illustrated by R. Gregory Christie and text by Anne Rockwell (Random House)

Virgie Goes to School with Us Boys illustrated by E. B. Lewis and text by Elizabeth Fitzgerald Howard (Simon & Schuster)

2000 Winners

Author Award Winner

Bud, Not Buddy by Christopher Paul Curtis (Delacorte)

Author Honor Books

Francie by Karen English (Farrar, Straus and Giroux)

Black Hands, White Sails: The Story of African-American Whalers by Patricia C. and Frederick L. McKissack (Scholastic Press)

Monster by Walter Dean Myers (HarperCollins)

Illustrator Award Winner

In the Time of the Drums illustrated by Brian Pinkney and text by Kim L. Siegelson (Jump at the Sun/Hyperion Books for Children)

Illustrator Honor Books

My Rows and Piles of Coins illustrated by E. B. Lewis and text by Tololwa M. Mollel (Clarion Books)

Black Cat by Christopher Myers (Scholastic)

1999 Winners

Author Award Winner

Heaven by Angela Johnson (Simon & Schuster)

Author Honor Books

Jazmin's Notebook by Nikki Grimes (Dial Books)

Breaking Ground, Breaking Silence: The Story of New York's African Burial Ground by Joyce Hansen and Gary McGowan (Henry Holt and Company)

The Other Side: Shorter Poems by Angela Johnson (Orchard Books)

Illustrator Award Winner

i see the rhythm illustrated by Michele Wood and text by Toyomi Igus (Children's Book Press)

Illustrator Honor Books

I Have Heard of a Land illustrated by Floyd Cooper and text by Joyce Carol Thomas (Joanna Cotler Books/HarperCollins)

The Bat Boy and His Violin illustrated by E. B. Lewis and text by Gavin Curtis (Simon & Schuster)

Duke Ellington: The Piano Prince and His Orchestra illustrated by Brian Pinkney and text by Andrea Davis Pinkney (Hyperion Books for Children)

1998 Winners

Author Award Winner

Forged by Fire by Sharon M. Draper (Atheneum)

Author Honor Books

Bayard Rustin: Behind the Scenes of the Civil Rights Movement by James Haskins (Hyperion)

I Thought My Soul Would Rise and Fly: The Diary of Patsy, a Freed Girl by Joyce Hansen (Scholastic)

Illustrator Award Winner

In Daddy's Arms I Am Tall: African Americans Celebrating Fathers illustrated by Javaka Steptoe and text by Alan Schroeder (Lee & Low)

Illustrator Honor Books

Ashley Bryan's ABC of African American Poetry by Ashley Bryan (Jean Karl/Atheneum)

Harlem illustrated by Christopher Myers and text by Walter Dean Myers (Scholastic)

The Hunterman and the Crocodile by Baba Wagué Diakité (Scholastic)

1997 Winners

Author Award Winner

Slam by Walter Dean Myers (Scholastic)

Author Honor Books

Rebels Against Slavery: American Slave Revolts by Patricia C. and Frederick L. McKissack (Scholastic)

Illustrator Award Winner

Minty: A Story of Young Harriet Tubman illustrated by Jerry Pinkney and text by Alan Schroeder (Dial Books for Young Readers)

Illustrator Honor Books

The Palm of My Heart: Poetry by African American Children illustrated by Gregorie Christie and edited by Davida Adedjouma (Lee & Low Books Inc.)

Running the Road to ABC illustrated by Reynold Ruffins and text by Denize Lauture (Simon & Schuster Books for Young Readers)

Neeny Coming, Neeny Going illustrated by Synthia Saint James and text by Karen English (BridgeWater Books)

1996 Winners

Author Award Winner

Her Stories by Virginia Hamilton (Scholastic/Blue Sky Press)

Author Honor Books

The Watsons Go to Birmingham—1963 by Christopher Paul Curtis (Delacorte)

Like Sisters on the Homefront by Rita Williams-Garcia (Delacorte)

From the Notebooks of Melanin Sun by Jacqueline Woodson (Scholastic/Blue Sky Press)

Illustrator Award Winner

The Middle Passage: White Ships/Black Cargo by Tom Feelings (Dial Books for Young Readers)

Illustrator Honor Books

Her Stories illustrated by Leo and Diane Dillon and text by Virginia Hamilton (Scholastic/Blue Sky Press)

The Faithful Friend illustrated by Brian Pinkney and text by Robert San Souci (Simon & Schuster Books for Young Readers)

1995 Winners

Author Award Winner

Christmas in the Big House, Christmas in the Quarters by Patricia C. and Frederick L. McKissack (Scholastic)

Author Honor Books

The Captive by Joyce Hansen (Scholastic)

I Hadn't Meant to Tell You This by Jacqueline Woodson (Delacorte)

Black Diamond: Story of the Negro Baseball Leagues by Patricia C. and
Frederick L. McKissack (Scholastic)

Illustrator Award Winner
The Creation illustrated by James Ransome and text by James Weldon
Johnson (Holiday House)

Illustrator Honor Books
The Singing Man illustrated by Terea Shaffer and text by Angela Shelf
Medearis (Holiday House)
Meet Danitra Brown illustrated by Floyd Cooper and text by Nikki Grimes
(Lothrop, Lee & Shepard)

1994 Winners

Author Award Winner
Toning the Sweep by Angela Johnson (Orchard)

Author Honor Books
Brown Honey in Broomwheat Tea by Joyce Carol Thomas and illustrated by
Floyd Cooper (HarperCollins)
Malcolm X: By Any Means Necessary by Walter Dean Myers (Scholastic)

Illustrator Award Winner
Soul Looks Back in Wonder illustrated by Tom Feelings and text edited by
Phyllis Fogelman (Dial Books for Young Readers)

Illustrator Honor Books
Brown Honey in Broomwheat Tea illustrated by Floyd Cooper and text by
Joyce Carol Thomas (HarperCollins)
Uncle Jed's Barbershop illustrated by James Ransome and text by Margaree
King Mitchell (Simon & Schuster)

1993 Winners

Author Award Winner
The Dark-Thirty: Southern Tales of the Supernatural by Patricia C. McKissack
(Knopf)

Author Honor Books
Mississippi Challenge by Mildred Pitts Walter (Bradbury)
Sojourner Truth: Ain't I a Woman? by Patricia C. and Frederick L. McKissack
(Scholastic)
Somewhere in the Darkness by Walter Dean Myers (Scholastic)

Illustrator Award Winner
The Origin of Life on Earth: An African Creation Myth illustrated by Kathleen
Atkins Wilson and retold by David A. Anderson/SANKOFA (Sights)

Illustrator Honor Books
Little Eight John illustrated by Wil Clay and text by Jan Wahl (Lodestar)
Sukey and the Mermaid illustrated by Brian Pinkney and text by Robert San
Souci (Four Winds)
Working Cotton illustrated by Carole Byard and text by Sherley Anne
Williams (Harcourt)

1992 Winners

Author Award Winner
Now Is Your Time! The African American Struggle for Freedom by Walter Dean Myers (HarperCollins)

Author Honor Books
Night on Neighborhood Street by Eloise Greenfield and illustrated by Jan Spivey Gilchrist (Dial)

Illustrator Award Winner
Tar Beach by Faith Ringgold (Crown)

Illustrator Honor Books
All Night, All Day: A Child's First Book of African American Spirituals illustrated and selected by Ashley Bryan (Atheneum)
Night on Neighborhood Street illustrated by Jan Spivey Gilchrist and text by Eloise Greenfield (Dial)

1991 Winners

Author Award Winner
The Road to Memphis by Mildred D. Taylor (Dial)

Author Honor Books
Black Dance in America by James Haskins (Crowell)
When I Am Old with You by Angela Johnson (Orchard)

Illustrator Award Winner
Aida illustrated by Leo and Diane Dillon and text by Leontyne Price (Harcourt)

1990 Winners

Author Award Winner
A Long Hard Journey: The Story of the Pullman Porter by Patricia C. and Frederick L. McKissack (Walker)

Author Honor Books
Nathaniel Talking by Eloise Greenfield and illustrated by Jan Spivey Gilchrist (Black Butterfly)
The Bells of Christmas by Virginia Hamilton (Harcourt)
Martin Luther King, Jr., and the Freedom Movement by Lillie Patterson (Facts on File)

Illustrator Award Winner
Nathaniel Talking illustrated by Jan Spivey Gilchrist and text by Eloise Greenfield (Black Butterfly)

Illustrator Honor Books
The Talking Eggs illustrated by Jerry Pinkney and text by Robert San Souci (Dial)

1989 Winners

Author Award Winner
Fallen Angels by Walter Dean Myers (Scholastic)

Author Honor Books
A Thief in the Village and Other Stories by James Berry (Orchard)
Anthony Burns: The Defeat and Triumph of a Fugitive Slave by Virginia
    Hamilton (Knopf)
Illustrator Award Winner
Mirandy and Brother Wind illustrated by Jerry Pinkney and text by Patricia
    C. McKissack (Knopf)
Illustrator Honor Books
Under the Sunday Tree illustrated by Amos Ferguson and text by Eloise
    Greenfield (Harper)
Storm in the Night illustrated by Pat Cummings and text by Mary Stolz
    (Harper)

1988 Winners

Author Award Winner
The Friendship by Mildred L. Taylor (Dial)

Author Honor Books
An Enchanted Hair Tale by Alexis De Veaux (Harper)
The Tales of Uncle Remus: The Adventures of Brer Rabbit by Julius Lester (Dial)

Illustrator Award Winner
Mufaro's Beautiful Daughters: An African Tale by John Steptoe (Lothrop)

Illustrator Honor Books
What a Morning! The Christmas Story in Black Spirituals illustrated by Ashley
    Bryan and selected by John Langstaff (Macmillan)
The Invisible Hunters: A Legend from the Miskito Indians of Nicaragua illus-
    trated by Joe Sam and compiled by Harriet Rohmer, Octavio Chow,
    and Morris Vidauro (Children's Press)

1987 Winners

Author Award Winner
Justin and the Best Biscuits in the World by Mildred Pitts Walter (Lothrop)

Author Honor Books
Lion and the Ostrich Chicks and Other African Folk Tales by Ashley Bryan
    (Atheneum)
Which Way Freedom by Joyce Hansen (Walker)

Illustrator Award Winner
Half a Moon and One Whole Star illustrated by Jerry Pinkney and text by
    Crescent Dragonwagon (Macmillan)

Illustrator Honor Books
Lion and the Ostrich Chicks and Other African Folk Tales by Ashley Bryan
    (Atheneum)
C.L.O.U.D.S. by Pat Cummings (Lothrop)

1986 Winners

Author Award Winner

The People Could Fly: American Black Folktales by Virginia Hamilton and illustrated by Leo and Diane Dillon (Knopf)

Author Honor Books

Junius Over Far by Virginia Hamilton (Harper)

Trouble's Child by Mildred Pitts Walter (Lothrop)

Illustrator Award Winner

The Patchwork Quilt illustrated by Jerry Pinkney and text by Valerie Flournoy (Dial)

Illustrator Honor Books

The People Could Fly: American Black Folktales illustrated by Leo and Diane Dillon and text by Virginia Hamilton (Knopf)

1985 Winners

Author Award Winner

Motown and Didi by Walter Dean Myers (Viking)

Author Honor Books

Circle of Gold by Candy Dawson Boyd (Apple/Scholastic)

A Little Love by Virginia Hamilton (Philomel)

Illustrator Award Winner

No award

1984 Winners

Author Award Winner

Everett Anderson's Goodbye by Lucille Clifton (Holt)

Special Citation:

The Words of Martin Luther King, Jr. compiled by Coretta Scott King (Newmarket Press)

Author Honor Books

The Magical Adventures of Pretty Pearl by Virginia Hamilton (Harper)

Lena Horne by James Haskins (Coward-McCann)

Bright Shadow by Joyce Carol Thomas (Avon)

Because We Are by Mildred Pitts Walter

Illustrator Award Winner

My Mama Needs Me illustrated by Pat Cummings and text by Mildred Pitts Walter (Lothrop)

1983 Winners

Author Award Winner

Sweet Whispers, Brother Rush by Virginia Hamilton (Philomel)

Author Honor Book

This Strange New Feeling by Julius Lester (Dial)

Illustrator Award Winner
Black Child by Peter Magubane (Knopf)

Illustrator Honor Books
All the Colors of the Race illustrated by John Steptoe and text by Arnold Adoff (Lothrop)

I'm Going to Sing: Black American Spirituals illustrated by Ashley Bryan (Atheneum)

Just Us Women illustrated by Pat Cummings and text by Jeanette Caines (Harper)

1982 Winners

Author Award Winner
Let the Circle Be Unbroken by Mildred D. Taylor (Dial)

Author Honor Books
Rainbow Jordan by Alice Childress (Coward-McCann)
Lou in the Limelight by Kristin Hunter (Scribner)
Mary: An Autobiography by Mary E. Mebane (Viking)

Illustrator Award Winner
Mother Crocodile: An Uncle Amadou Tale from Senegal illustrated by John Steptoe and text by Rosa Guy (Delacorte)

Illustrator Honor Book
Daydreamers illustrated by Tom Feelings and text by Eloise Greenfield (Dial)

1981 Winners

Author Award Winner
This Life by Sidney Poitier (Knopf)

Author Honor Book
Don't Explain: A Song of Billie Holiday by Alexis De Veaux (Harper)

Illustrator Award Winner
Beat the Story Drum, Pum-Pum by Ashley Bryan (Atheneum)

Illustrator Honor Books
Grandmama's Joy illustrated by Carole Byard and text by Eloise Greenfield (Collins)

Count on Your Fingers African Style illustrated by Jerry Pinkney and text by Claudia Zaslavsky (Crowell)

1980 Winners

Author Award Winner
The Young Landlords by Walter Dean Myers (Viking)

Author Honor Books
Movin' Up by Berry Gordy (Harper)
Childtimes: A Three-Generation Memoir by Eloise Greenfield and Lessie Jones Little (Harper)
Andrew Young: Young Man with a Mission by James Haskins (Lothrop)

James Van Der Zee: The Picture Takin' Man by James Haskins (Dodd)
Let the Lion Eat Straw by Ellease Southerland (Scribner)
Illustrator Award Winner
Cornrows illustrated by Carole Byard and text by Camille Yarborough
  (Coward-McCann)

1979 Winners

Author Award Winner
Escape to Freedom by Ossie Davis (Viking)

Author Honor Books
Benjamin Banneker by Lillie Patterson (Abingdon)
I Have a Sister, My Sister Is Deaf by Jeanne W. Peterson (Harper)
Justice and Her Brothers by Virginia Hamilton (Greenwillow)
Skates of Uncle Richard by Carol Fenner (Random)

Illustrator Award Winner
Something on My Mind illustrated by Tom Feelings and text by Nikki
  Grimes (Dial)

1978 Winners

Author Award Winner
Africa Dream by Eloise Greenfield and illustrated by Carole Bayard
  (Crowell)

Author Honor Books
The Days When the Animals Talked: Black Folk Tales and How They Came to Be
  by William J. Faulkner (Follett)
Marvin and Tige by Frankcina Glass (St. Martin's)
Mary McCleod Bethune by Eloise Greenfield (Crowell)
Barbara Jordan by James Haskins (Dial)
Coretta Scott King by Lillie Patterson (Garrard)
*Portia: The Life of Portia Washington Pittman, the Daughter of Booker T.
  Washington* by Ruth Ann Stewart (Doubleday)

Illustrator Award Winner
Africa Dream illustrated by Carole Bayard and text by Eloise Greenfield
  (Crowell)

1977 Winners

Author Award Winner
The Story of Stevie Wonder by James Haskins (Lothrop)
Illustrator Award Winner
No award

1976 Winners

Author Award Winner
Duey's Tale by Pearl Bailey (Harcourt)
Illustrator Award Winner
No award

1975 Winners
Author Award Winner
The Legend of Africana by Dorothy Robinson (Johnson)
Illustrator Award Winner
No award

1974 Winners
Author Award Winner
Ray Charles by Sharon Bell Mathis and illustrated by George Ford (Crowell)
Illustrator Award Winner
Ray Charles illustrated by George Ford and text by Sharon Bell Mathis
   (Crowell)
(Note: Prior to 1974, the Coretta Scott King Award was given to authors only)

1973 Winner
I Never Had It Made: The Autobiography of Jackie Robinson as told to Alfred
   Duckett (Putnam)

1972 Winner
17 Black Artists by Elton C. Fax (Dodd)

1971 Winner
Black Troubador: Langston Hughes by Charlemae Rollins (Rand McNally)

1970 Winner
Martin Luther King, Jr.: Man of Peace by Lillie Patterson (Garrard)

Glossary

Accuracy   The degree to which a reader can identify words in text correctly or with precision (e.g., a skilled reader reads with a high level of accuracy).

Antiphonal reading   A version of choral reading in which students take turns reading aloud parts from a practiced text; for example, reading dialogue or poetry written for multiple voices. This practice can also be used for pairs of readers.

Automaticity   The instantaneous recognition of words in text without conscious effort or attention; a skilled reader achieves automaticity with the vast majority of words encountered while reading.

Basal reader   A collection of stories—often written to meet specific instructional goals and including an accompanying teacher's guide and supplemental materials—that frequently serves as the basis of a school's reading curriculum.

Book-handling knowledge   The awareness that the reading of books involves certain conventions (e.g., the understanding that print carries meaning, that the book is read from the front to back. It is important to note that these conventions can vary in different cultures, for example, text is read from left to right in English but from top to bottom in Chinese; also, see *concepts of print*).

Challenging text   Text that would be at a learner's frustration level if significant support or scaffolding were not provided; in general, it is seen to be text that has an 85 to 90 percent accuracy level upon a student's first reading.

Choral reading   The instructional approach in which both the students and the teacher read a text aloud in unison.

Combat reading   A version of round-robin reading in which students look for other students who are off-task and choose them as the next person to read aloud.

Concepts of print   Understandings about written language such as the notion that words are comprised of letters and are separated from one another by the spaces that surround them, that punctuation represents prosodic elements, etc. (also see *book-handling knowledge*).

Connected text   Written texts (e.g., books, poems, newspaper or magazine articles) as opposed to decontextualized words (e.g., words in isolation or in random lists).

Correct words per minute (cwpm)   The number of words a person is able to read correctly in a one-minute period.

Echo reading   The instructional approach in which the teacher reads a section (several sentences or paragraphs) of a text aloud and the students respond by reading it back in unison.

Emergent readers   Young children who are making discoveries about print and texts (e.g., the development of alphabet knowledge, phonemic awareness, concepts of print) prior to the beginnings of conventional reading instruction.

Expository texts   Texts written with the purpose of providing the reader with knowledge or information.

Flexible grouping   The use of a variety of grouping formats (e.g., heterogeneous and homogeneous; individuals; pairs of learners; or small and large groups) depending on both the task and the needs of the learners.

Fluency   See *fluent reading*.

Fluent reading   Reading that incorporates automatic as well as accurate word recognition along with the use of appropriate phrasing and expression.

Frustration level   A text that is too difficult for a learner to read successfully even with the use of instructional support or scaffolding.

Grade-level texts   Texts that are considered to be appropriate for use in a particular grade based on expectations for that grade or a readability formula.

High-frequency words   Words that appear significantly more frequently in text and speech than do most other words (e.g., *the, and, in*).

Independent level   A text that an individual can read successfully without any assistance or scaffolding.

Informal Reading Inventory (IRI)   The use of increasingly difficult passages of text as a means of determining a learner's independent, instructional, and frustration reading level; such assessments do not follow a standardized protocol for administration.

Instructional level   A text that a learner can read successfully when provided with standard levels of classroom instruction or scaffolding.

Letter-sound correspondence   The relationship between a letter or letters and the sound(s) it represents, for example, the letter *c* can represent /k/ (e.g., *colt*) and /s/ (e.g., *center*).

Literature anthology   A collection of children's literature at a particular grade level; unlike older basal readers, however, the stories do not have a controlled vocabulary and are not written to meet specific instructional goals.

Miscues   An oral response that differs from a written word (e.g., a student reads *cat* for *car* or *house* for *home*) and that provides insight into an individual's reading strategies.

Mumble reading   An oral reading approach in which reading is performed so quietly that it sounds like mumbling to a passerby. However, students who read in this manner need to articulate the words clearly; the term *mumble* simply refers to the level of noise associated with such oral reading.

Narrative texts   Texts written to tell a story, whether fiction or nonfiction (e.g., a biography).

Parsing   Breaking a sentence into appropriate phrase units as an aid to comprehension.

Partner reading   The instructional approach in which a pair of readers (two students or a teacher/tutor and a student) take turns reading sections of a text, alternating roles between reader and listener/supporter.

Phonemic awareness   The insight that spoken words are composed of individual, and somewhat separable, sounds.

Popcorn reading   A version of round-robin reading in which students are randomly selected to read a small section of text aloud.

Popsicle reading   A version of round-robin reading in which students' names are written on popsicle sticks and then randomly selected in order to determine the next person to read aloud.

Prosody   The aspects of reading such as stress, emphasis, and appropriate phrasing that, when taken together, create an expressive rendering of a text.

Reading rate   How quickly an individual reads, either silently or orally; reading rate is often expressed in terms of *words read per minute* or *correct words read per minute* and can be compared to norms for grade and time of year as part of a broader evaluation of reading fluency.

Round-robin reading   A procedure in which students read aloud short passages of text in a predetermined order.

Running record   An assessment procedure in which a student's reading is evaluated using text(s) that the student is currently reading in order to determine facility of reading, to analyze miscues, and to evaluate the use of strategies. Can also be used to determine a student's reading level.

Scaffolded reading strategies   Approaches to reading instruction that provide students with support, allowing them to engage in learning that would otherwise be beyond their ability.

Scaffolded wide reading   The reading of a wide variety of texts with significant support, usually in the form of echo, choral, or partner reading.

Scaffolding   Instructional support designed to help learners undertake tasks that they would be unable to complete independently.

Shared reading   The use of a shared text as the basis of instruction for a group of learners in order to develop a common understanding about a topic or strategy.

Sight vocabulary   All the words that an individual can recognize automatically, without relying on analysis for identification.

Sight word   Any word that an individual can recognize automatically (not to be confused with *high-frequency words*).

Summer slump   The loss in learning that occurs for many students between the end of one school year and the start of the next.

Trade book   A book that is available for sale to the general public as opposed to one written specifically for use in the classroom (i.e., a textbook).

Unison reading   See *choral reading*.

Whisper reading   An oral reading approach in which a learner reads aloud quietly, in a manner that resembles whispering, in order to keep from disturbing others in the room.

Word recognition   The identification of words, whether in isolation or in context, in order to determine pronunciation and meaning.

Words per minute (wpm)   The total number of words a person reads in a minute regardless of the accuracy of the reading.

References

Adams, M. J. (1990). *Beginning to read: Thinking and learning about print*. Cambridge, MA: MIT Press.

Allington, R. L. (1977). If they don't read much, how they ever gonna get good? *Journal of Reading, 21,* 57–61.

Allington, R. L. (1983). Fluency: The neglected reading goal. *The Reading Teacher, 36,* 556–561.

Allington, R. L. (2001). *What really matters for struggling readers: Designing research-based programs.* New York: Longman.

Allington, R. L. (2005, June). *What do good literacy programs look like?* Paper presented at the International Reading Association's urban dean's network.

Anderson, R. C., Wilson, P. T., & Fielding, L. G. (1988). Growth in reading and how children spend their time outside of school. *Reading Research Quarterly, 23,* 285–303.

Ash, G. E., & Kuhn, M. R. (2006). Meaningful oral and silent reading in the elementary and middle school classroom: Breaking the Round-Robin Reading addiction. In T. Rasinski, C. Blachowicz & K. Lems (Eds.), *Fluency instruction: Research-based best practices* (pp. 155–172). New York: The Guilford Press.

Averill, E. (1988). *The fire cat.* New York: HarperCollins.

Betts, E. A. (1946). *Foundations of reading instruction.* New York: American Book Co.

Bidwell, S. M. (1990). Using drama to increase motivation, comprehension, and fluency. *Journal of Reading, 34,* 38–41.

Bonsall, C. (1982). *The case of the dumb bells.* New York: HarperCollins.

Bridwell, N. (1997). *Clifford the big red dog.* New York: Scholastic.

Cannon, J. (1993). *Stellaluna.* New York: Scholastic.

Carroll, L. (2006). *Alice's adventures in wonderland and through the looking glass.* New York: Bantam Books.

Cassidy, J., & Cassidy, D. (2007, February). What's hot, what's not for 2007. *Reading Today, 24*(4), 1.

Casteel, C. A. (1988). Effects of chunked reading among learning disabled students: An experimental comparison of computer and traditional chunked passages. *Journal of Educational Technology Systems, 17*(2), 115–121.

Chall, J. S. (1996). *Stages of reading development.* (2nd ed.). Fort Worth, TX: Harcourt-Brace.

Chomsky, C. (1976). After decoding: What? *Language Arts, 53,* 288–296.

Clay, M. M. (2006). *An observation survey of early literacy achievement, 2nd ed.* Portsmouth, NH: Heinemann.

Cooper, J. D., & Kiger, N. D. (2005). *Literacy: Helping children construct meaning, 6th ed.* New York: Houghton Mifflin.

Cromer, W. (1970). The difference model: A new explanation for some reading difficulties. *Journal of Educational Psychology, 61,* 471–483.

Dahl, P. R. (1979). An experimental program for teaching high speed word recognition and comprehension skills. In J. E. Button, T. Lovitt & T. Rowland (Eds.), *Communications research in learning disabilities and mental retardation* (pp. 33–65) Baltimore: University Park Press.

Dowhower, S. L. (1989). Repeated reading: Research into practice. *The Reading Teacher, 42,* 502–507.

Erekson, J. (2003, May). *Prosody: The problem of expression in fluency.* Paper presented at the annual meeting of the International Reading Association, Orlando, FL.

Fountas, I. C., & Pinnell, G. S. (1999). *Matching books to readers: Using leveled books in guided reading, K–3.* Portsmouth, NH: Heinemann.

Fountas, I. C., & Pinnell, G. S. (2005). *The Fountas & Pinnell leveled book list, K–8.* Portsmouth, NH: Heinemann.

Gambrell, L. B. (1984). How much time do children spend reading during teacher-directed reading instruction? In J. A. Niles & L. A. Harris (Eds.), *Changing perspectives on research in reading/language processing and instruction, Thirty-third yearbook of the National Reading Conference* (pp. 193–198). Rochester, NY: National Reading Conference.

Gunning, T. G. (1997). *Best books for beginning readers.* Boston: Allyn & Bacon.

Gunning, T. G. (2002). *Building Literacy in the Content Areas.* New York: Allyn & Bacon.

Hasbrouck, J. E. (2006, Summer). Drop everything and read—but how? *American Educator.* Available at: www.aft.org/pubs-reports/american_educator/issues/summer06/fluency.htm.

Hasbrouck, J. E., & Tindal, G. (1992). Curriculum-based oral reading fluency norms for students in grades 2 through 5. *Teaching Exceptional Children, 24*, 41–44.

Heckelman, R. G. (1969). A neurological-impress method of remedial-reading instruction. *Academic Therapy Quarterly, 4*, 277–282.

Heckelman, R. G. (1986). N.I.M. revisited. *Academic Therapy, 21*, 411–420.

Henning, K. (1974). Drama reading, an on-going classroom activity at the elementary school level. *Elementary English, 51*, 48–51.

Hoffman, J. V. (1987). Rethinking the role of oral reading in basal instruction. *TheElementary School Journal, 87*, 367–373.

Hoffman, J. V., & Crone, S. (1985). The oral recitation lesson: A research-derived strategy for reading basal texts. In J. A. Niles & R. V. Lalik (Eds.), *Issues in literacy: A research perspective, Thirty-fourth yearbook of the National Reading Conference* (pp. 76–83). Rochester, NY: National Reading Conference.

Hollingsworth, P. M. (1970). An experiment with the impress method of teaching reading. *The Reading Teacher, 24*, 112–114.

Hollingsworth, P. M. (1978). An experimental approach to the impress method of teaching reading. *The Reading Teacher, 31*, 624–626.

Hoyt, L. (2000). *Snapshots: Literacy minilessons up close*. Portsmouth, NH: Heinemann.

Keats, E. J. (1977). *Whistle for Willie*. New York: Puffin Books USA.

Koskinen, P. S., & Blum, I. H. (1984). Repeated oral reading and the acquisition of fluency. In J. A. Niles & L. A. Harris (Eds.), *Changing perspectives on research in reading/language processing and instruction: Thirty-third yearbook of the National Reading Conference* (pp. 183–187). Rochester, NY: National Reading Conference.

Koskinen, P. S., & Blum, I. H. (1986). Paired repeated reading: A classroom strategy for developing fluent reading. *The Reading Teacher, 40*, 70–75.

Kuhn, M. R. (2005). A comparative study of small-group fluency instruction. *Reading Psychology, 26*, 127–146.

Kuhn, M. R. (2007). Effective oral reading assessment (or why round-robin reading doesn't cut it). In J. R. Paratore & R. L. McCormack (Eds.), *Classroom literacy assessment: Making sense of what students know and do*. New York: The Guilford Press.

Kuhn, M .R., & Schwanenflugel, P. J. (2006). Fluency-Oriented Reading Instruction: A merging of theory and practice. In K. A. D. Stahl &

M. C. McKenna (Eds.), *Reading research at work: Foundations of effective practice* (pp. 205–213). New York: The Guilford Press.

Kuhn, M. R., Schwanenflugel, P. J., Morris, R. D., Morrow, L. M., Woo, D. G. Meisinger, E. B., Sevcik, R. A., Bradley, B. A., & Stahl, S. A. (in memoriam). (2006). Teaching children to become fluent and automatic readers. *Journal of Literacy Research, 38*, 357–387.

Kuhn, M. R., & Stahl, S. A. (2003). Fluency: A review of developmental and remedial practices. *The Journal of Educational Psychology, 95*, 3–21.

Labbo, L. D., & Teale, W. H. (1990). Cross-age reading: A strategy for helping poor readers. *The Reading Teacher, 43*, 362–369.

LaBerge, D., & Samuels, S. J. (1974). Toward a theory of automatic information processing in reading. *Cognitive Psychology, 6*, 293–323.

Leslie, L., & Caldwell, J. (1995). *Qualitative reading inventory–II*. Boston: Longman.

Lobel, A. (1970). *Frog and Toad are friends*. New York: HarperCollins.

Logan, G. D. (1997). Automaticity and reading: Perspectives from the instance theory of automaticity. *Reading & Writing Quarterly: Overcoming Learning Difficulties, 13*, 123–146.

Martin, A. M. (1995). *Kristy's great idea (The baby-sitters club #1)*. New York: Scholastic.

McKenna, M. C., & Stahl, S. A. (2003). *Assessment for reading instruction*. New York: The Guilford Press.

Meisinger, E. B., & Bradley, B. A. (2007). Classroom practices for supporting fluency development. In M. R. Kuhn & P. J. Schwanenflugel (Eds.), *Fluency in the classroom*. New York: The Guilford Press.

Miller, J., & Schwanenflugel, P. J. (2006). Prosody of syntactically complex sentences in the oral reading of young children. *Journal of Educational Psychology, 98*, 839–843.

Morris, D., & Nelson, L. (1992). Supported oral reading with low achieving second graders. *Reading Research and Instruction, 32*, 49–63.

Mostow, J., & Beck, J. (2005, June). *Micro-analysis of fluency gains in a reading tutor that listens*. Paper presented at the Society for the Scientific Study of Reading, Toronto, Canada.

National Center for Education Statistics. (1995). *Listening to children read aloud, 15*. NAEP's oral reading fluency scale. Washington, DC: U.S. Department of Education, National Center for Education Statistics.

National Reading Panel. (2000). *Teaching children to read: An evidence-based assessment of the scientific research literature on reading and its implications for reading instruction. Reports of the subgroups.* (NIH Publication No. 00-4754). Washington, DC: U.S. Government Printing Office.

O'Shea, L. J., Sindelar, P. T., & O'Shea, D. (1985). The effects of repeated readings and attentional cues on reading fluency and comprehension. *Journal of Reading Behavior, 17,* 129–142.

O'Shea, L. J., Sindelar, P. T., & O'Shea, D. (1987). The effects of repeated readings and attentional cues on the reading fluency and comprehension of learning disabled readers. *Learning Disabilities Research, 2*(2), 103–109.

Pikulski, J. J., & Chard, D. J. (2005). Fluency: Bridge between decoding and reading comprehension. *Reading Teacher, 58,* 510–519.

Rasinski, T. V. (2003). *The fluent reader: Oral reading strategies for building word recognition, fluency, and comprehension.* New York: Scholastic.

Rasinski, T. V. (2004). *Assessing reading fluency.* Honolulu: Pacific Resources for Education and Learning. Available at: www.prel.org/products/re_/assessing-fluency.htm.

Rasinski, T. V. (2006). A brief history of reading fluency. In S. J. Samuels & A. E. Farstrup (Eds.), *What research has to say about fluency instruction.* Newark, DE: International Reading Association.

Rasinski, T. V., Padak, N., Linek, W., & Sturtevant, E. (1994). Effects of fluency development on urban second-grade readers. *Journal of Educational Research, 87,* 158–165.

Rey, H. A. (1973). *Curious George.* New York: Houghton Mifflin.

Samuels, S. J. (1979). The method of repeated readings. *The Reading Teacher, 32,* 403–408.

Schwanenflugel, P. J., Kuhn, M. R., Morris, R. D., Morrow, L. M., Meisinger, E., Woo, D. G., & Quirk, M. (under review). Insights into fluency instruction: Short- and long-term effects of two reading programs. *Reading Research and Instruction.*

Schwebel, E. A. (2007). A comparative study of small group fluency instruction—a replication and extension of Kuhn's (2005) study. Unpublished master's thesis, Kean University, Union, NJ.

Shanahan, T. (2007). Differentiating instruction when embedding literacy. Invited speaker at the 39th Annual Conference on Reading and Writing. Rutgers Centre for Effective School Practices. April 20, 2007. Somerset, NJ.

Stahl, S. A., & Heubach, K. M. (2005). Fluency-oriented reading instruction. *Journal of Literacy Research, 37,* 25–60.

Stanovich, K. E. (1986). Matthew effects in reading: Some consequences of individual differences in the acquisition of literacy. *Reading Research Quarterly, 21,* 360–407.

Stroud, J. (2006). *The Bartimaeus trilogy boxed set.* New York: Mirimax Books/Hyperion for Children.

Teale, W. H., & Sulzby, E. (1986). *Emergent literacy: Writing and reading.* New York: Ablex.

Truss, L. (2004). *Eats, shoots, and leaves: The zero tolerance approach to punctuation.* New York: Gotham Books.

Valencia, S. W., Smith, A., Reece, A., Newman, H., Wixson, K., & Li, M. (2005). The rush for oral reading fluency: Issues of assessment and implications for instruction. Paper presented at the Berkeley Summer Literacy Institute, UC Berkeley, Berkeley, CA.

Walczyk, J. J., Marsiglia, C. S., Johns, A. K., & Bryan, K. S. (2004). Children's compensations for poorly automated reading skills. *Discourse Processes: A Multidisciplinary Journal, 37,* 47–66.

Walker, B. J., Mokhtari, K., & Sargent, S. (2006). Reading fluency: More than fast and accurate reading. In T. Rasinski, C. Blachowicz, & K. Lems (Eds.). *Fluency instruction: Research-based best practices.* New York: The Guilford Press.

Weiss, D. S. (1983). The effects of text segmentation on children's reading comprehension. *Discourse Processes, 6*(1), 77–89.

Yopp, R. H., & Yopp, H. K. (2000). Supporting phonemic awareness development in the classroom. *The Reading Teacher, 54,* 130–143.

Zutell, J., & Rasinski, T. V. (1991). Training teachers to attend to their students' oral reading fluency. *Theory into Practice, 30,* 211–217.

Index

Neurological Impress Method (NIM), 88–90
summary, 79
Norms for correct words per minute, 31

O

One-on-one instruction, 80–82
Oral reading
changing role of, 12–13
choral reading, 18–19
echo reading, 16–17
lesson plans, 65–67
NAEP Fluency Scale, 33–34
partner reading, 20–22
place in curriculum, 9
recording for evaluation, 37
round-robin reading, 9–12
supported, 73–75
unpracticed text, 81
Oral Recitation Lesson (ORL), 63–67
Orthography, 6
O'Shea, Dorothy, 84
O'Shea, Lawrence, 84

P

Pacific Resources for Education and Learning (PREL), 30
Paired repeated reading, 102–105
summary, 101
Parsing, 7
Partner reading
about, 1
and fluency instruction, 20–22, 45
and Fluency-Oriented Oral Reading (FOOR), 72
and Fluency-Oriented Reading Instruction (FORI), 61
scaffolding, 111
text type, 112
and Wide Fluency-Oriented Reading Instruction (Wide FORI), 56
Phonemic awareness, 2
Phones (PVC pipe), 45, 76, 94
Phrase organization, 8
and fluency instruction, 15
Phrasing
and assessment, 26

and comprehension, 15
importance of, 33
and paired repeated readings, 103
and small-group instruction, 63
Podcasts, 45
and reading-while-listening method, 93
Popcorn reading
as alternative to round-robin reading, 11–12
description, 12
Popsicle reading
as alternative to round-robin reading, 11–12
description, 12
Practice
and automaticity, 6
and evaluation, 27
and Fluency Development Lesson (FDL), 105
and fluency instruction, 14
and small-group instruction, 63
Prosody
development of, 3
evaluating, 32–36
and fluency, 6–8
and fluency instruction, 15
and Fluency-Oriented Oral Reading (FOOR), 70
and Oral Recitation Lesson (ORL), 66
and repeated readings, 83
and supported wide reading, 43
Punctuation, and prosody, 6–7

Q

Qualitative Reading Inventory (QRI), 47

R

Rasinski, Tim, 12, 30
fluency principles, 35, 105
Reader's theater, 108–111
summary, 101
Reading development, 2–3
effective strategies, 14–15
Reading instruction history, 12–13
Reading material. See Text type

Reading rate
and assessment, 26
and Fluency Development Lesson (FDL), 106
and paired repeated readings, 103
and reading-while-listening method, 92
and repeated readings, 43, 84
Reading selection. See Challenging text; Text type
Reading-while-listening, 91–94
summary, 79
Repetition, 42
effectiveness, 84
and individual instruction, 79
lesson plans, 85–88
for one or two students, 80, 82–85
and Oral Recitation Lesson (ORL), 63
Paired repeated reading, 102–105
vs. scaffolded wide reading, 42–44, 67–71
and whole-class instruction, 58
Round-robin reading, 9–12
alternative approaches, 63
ineffectiveness, 42
Running record, 76

S

Samuels, Jay, 43, 82
Scaffolding
about, 42
and challenging texts, 44–45
and choral reading, 18
and echo reading, 16
and fluency instruction, 16–17
for Fluency-Oriented Reading Instruction (FORI), 46
and Oral Recitation Lesson (ORL), 63
and partner reading, 20
and repetition, 43
vs. repetition, 42–44, 67–71
and small-group instruction, 63
and supported oral reading, 73
and type of reading instruction, 111
and use of challenging material, 45